THE
CHERRY
ON TOP

WHAT ADDS
VALUE

STEVE GILLILAND

PEARHOUSE
PRESS

Published by Pearhouse Press, Pittsburgh, Pennsylvania

Printed in the United States of America.

ISBN: 9781732006935

LCCN: 2019936341

This publication is designed to provide accurate and authoritative information in regard to the subject matter covered. It is sold with the understanding that the publisher is not engaged in rendering legal, accounting, or other professional services. If legal advice or other expert assistance is required, the services of a competent professional person should be sought.

Cover Design: Mike Urbowicz
Dust Jacket & Book Layout: Mike Murray

IN LOVING MEMORY
OF MY MOTHER

Life doesn't come with an instruction
manual. It comes with a *mother*.

Thank you, Mother, for showing me
strengths I didn't know I had, and how to
deal with fears I never knew existed.

You added so much value to my life!

Patricia L. Wise
1937 – 2021

3 JOHN 1:4 KJV
*"I have no greater joy than to hear that
my children walk in truth."*

CONTACT

CALL

866-445-5452 TOLL-FREE

724-540-5019 DIRECT

EMAIL

steve@stevegilliland.com

VISIT

www.stevegilliland.com

This book is dedicated to my wife Diane,
whose countless qualities have added
so much value to my life.

ACKNOWLEDGMENTS

This book is a tribute to all the people who have contributed to my life in a meaningful and positive way. To everyone who gave more than they took, and taught me things I didn't know. To the individuals who introduced me to people who added value to my life, and took me places I had never been.

CONTENTS

STEVE GILLILAND

INTRODUCTION

WHAT ADDS VALUE?

W e all have different measures and interpretations of what it means to be successful, and no one definition is right or wrong. We're all familiar with the common success factors; however, the number one thing you can do to ensure success – personally and professionally – is add value.

Value itself is something that is defined by your customers and the people in your life, not you. It doesn't matter what you think is valuable; if the people you are trying to win over don't see the value in what you're doing, then there is none. Everyone is different; therefore, the topic of value is highly subjective. While what you

1

have to offer may not be valued by everyone, there is likely a group of people who are dying to know or see what you have to offer.

How you can add value will differ from customer to customer and from person to person. The point is to remember that it is your customers or other people who dictate what's valuable, not you. We've all been taught that the thought behind a gift is what's most important. If your focus when giving a gift is really on the recipient and not on yourself, then you want to give them something they want and can use, appreciate and admire.

There are several ways you can add value in all areas of your life, and the things you do or offer need not be huge or earth shattering. Many truly valuable things are not.

Find out who your customer is and ask them what they want. Yes, ask them. Get to know your friends and family by asking what they want. Yes, ask them. Ask them about their fears, their desires or what that one thing is that would make their lives easier. Building a product, creating a report or finishing a chore might make you feel great, but if it's never used or valued, is it really worth it? Could your efforts be better focused elsewhere?

While you go through your day, ask yourself, *Am I adding value?* When was the last time you did something incredibly useful and were accessible, approachable and helpful? There are a number of things we can do to add value every day. To be effective at it, we need to get out of our heads, step away from our agendas and see what we can bring to our customers, friends and family.

You don't have to create something new to stand out; improve and offer more than what is already available. What makes a person choose one restaurant over the other? Is it the advertising, marketing or a person commenting about it? When you offer something better than what already exists, you get people talking.

Ever been to Barclay Prime in Philadelphia and ordered their $100 cheesesteak? They start with a fresh, house-made brioche roll brushed with homemade mustard. Then they add thinly sliced Kobe beef, marbleized onions, shaved heirloom tomatoes and triple Taleggio cheese. All of this is topped off with shaved, hand-harvested black truffles and butter-poached Maine lobster tail. They throw in a chilled split of champagne, and they not only add value, they stand out.

In the workplace, from an employer's point of view, it's possible that after the interview process they may be faced with having to make a hard choice between applicants who all meet the requirements of the job. At this juncture, they begin to review the applicants and look for the one who offered something additional to the required mix of skill, experience, background and temperament.

A lot of books have been written about success, and a lot of people believe they are successful because they have everything they want. They have added value to themselves. I believe significance comes when you add value to others. You can't have true success without significance.

This book is about understanding how important it is to develop and deliver value in everything you do. Great companies with great cultures add value to their people, products and services. This book is about recognizing the many things that add value and are worth more than what you perceive has merit.

STEVE GILLILAND

ACCEPTANCE

**SERENITY COMES WHEN YOU TRADE
EXPECTATIONS FOR ACCEPTANCE.**

In Buddhist philosophy, suffering = pain x resistance. Fundamentally, accepting the "pain" causes less suffering than struggling uselessly against it. We all have a choice to either accept or reject, and most of the time denying doesn't change our reality – it just causes more discomfort.

Acceptance doesn't mean you like, want or support whatever it is you're accepting. Instead, it is avoiding undue suffering. It doesn't mean you've chosen to endorse what you're accepting. It merely means you are choosing to allow its presence because you can't change it at that moment. The pain will still be there, but some of the sufferings will be alleviated.

It's rare that we would choose to accept our emotional or physical pain; therefore, we must remind ourselves that acceptance is an active process that must be practiced consciously. It will be frustrating at times, but with repetition it will begin to occur subconsciously. There will be times when you waver between acceptance and resistance; however, in time your inner opponent will diminish.

Acceptance is not apathy! It isn't a sign of weakness or surrendering. It's not a signal that you are giving up. It is an indication that you need to make a change, and you will make a change. Where you are will not last forever. You can accept your body and still change it, accept your emotions and acknowledge they're impermanent, and accept your behavior knowing you can change it tomorrow. Acceptance can be practiced in your appearance, your emotions, your health, your past, your thoughts or other individuals.

Thirteen years later, the relationship I have with my stepsons is far from what it used to be. I wouldn't say it's due entirely to acceptance, but it does show that acceptance doesn't always mean whatever you're accepting will be that way forever.

IT IS MUCH HEALTHIER TO FOCUS YOUR ACCEPTANCE ON THE PRESENT ALONGSIDE A REALISTIC REGARD FOR THE FUTURE.

I didn't endorse everything my stepsons were doing, but I recognized I couldn't change the current situation; therefore, I managed my anxiety knowing that things would change.

Learn to accept yourself and your reality. The value of accepting the reality of your life sounds like it should be easy. Many people hold onto regrets, disappointments and denial, though. When you fail to connect with reality, you end up having more than one size of jeans in your closet. It is imperative that you give up the fictional version of your life and learn to accept yourself, your life and your reality. Even if your situation is terrible, the first step toward improving it is acknowledging it for what it is.

Acknowledge all of yourself – the good, the bad, the ugly and, most importantly, the things that need improvement. For most of us, self-acceptance can be hard. We tend to be critical of ourselves, but there are a number of ways to learn to accept yourself and your life. Be honest with yourself and accept your current situation. Acknowledging your reality and admitting your deception is the key to creating a new future. The value of acceptance is realizing that dealing with the bad stuff is a way to get to the good stuff.

Accept what is, let go of what was and have faith in what will be. You don't need whipped cream and nuts to add a cherry.

ACTION

**THE BEST WAY TO GET SOMETHING
DONE IS TO BEGIN.**

Good things come to those who go, not wait! "To-do" lists are straightforward: they are the tasks you plan to accomplish during any given day or week. Few things are more satisfying to my wife than drawing a line through each entry. Many times, though, her anxiety increases when they inflate to impractical levels, and she ends up feeling overwhelmed and ineffective. This overwhelming feeling stops a lot of people from taking action.

One fundamental to taking action is to stop looking into the future trying to guess what's going to happen or not happen. Go with the flow, trust your heart, take action, learn and grow. Cut back on planning too far ahead making future decisions prior to being able to see things from a whole new perspective. As you move forward, the pieces of the puzzle usually fall into place when they need to, and with each piece you see more and more of the bigger picture. You don't have to know everything to know enough. Setting a goal is all well and good, but it should never be the reason you delay taking action. The goal is the target, but you always need to be focused on what you can do now.

The most effective way to effortlessly take action is to immediately take a small step. When you are planning, and trying to avoid mistakes that you haven't yet made, ask yourself what the next smallest step is that you can take in the direction of your goal.

Another way to take action is to see the end first. Instead of beating yourself up over striking out, envision hitting a home run. Everyone has experienced the unpleasant, uncomfortable and unwanted. This is why you have to see the end first and then take a small step. When you picture what you want and imagine you can attain it, you will come to expect it. This rehearsal will move you effortlessly in the right direction without the presence of fear or anxiety. This doesn't mean you will never feel negative, because as sure as I am sipping on

THERE WILL ALWAYS BE UNCERTAINTY. WITHOUT IT, POSSIBILITY CAN'T EXIST.

a scotch as I write this, you will. However, it will get you moving, and once you're moving, you become more relentless.

So, how do you write a book? You start to take action. The more I write, the quicker I write, and the combination of several small steps builds momentum. Energy is created from energy. Once I laid the groundwork to write this book, I began to focus on the productive actions that carry the most power and inspire the most significant results. Furthermore, I identify action steps that I need to take daily, weekly and monthly. Writing a book is the same principle as losing weight. To achieve either of these goals you must realize it is a process, not a single action. Every book I have written has required consistent effort, specific action steps taken day after day, week after week and month after month.

My actions keep my objectives moving forward, and my daily activity of writing a single page every morning holds the power of duplication and accumulation. Weekly actions such as reviewing and researching take a little longer to complete and involve an element of uncertainty when the results don't exactly match the expectations. Monthly actions are things you do to keep yourself on track, including evaluating your progress and readjusting your plans, if necessary. Monthly actions can also include unrelated activities not critical to your goal except in outlying ways.

It is worth noting that you are not planning a schedule, but rather identifying key action steps that you can do on a daily, weekly and monthly basis. Don't get caught up wondering how you can find time to do all this, or whether a specific task should be done daily or weekly. Simply make a list of the most productive actions you can think of with the belief that you can always add or change it later on.

It's time to add value and get moving!

ADAPTABILITY

LIKE MUSIC, LIFE MUST BE COMPOSED OF FEELING AND INSTINCT, NOT BY RULE.

A daptability is one of the top skills sought after by employers, and society demands proficiency in this area. Your ability to manage multiple obligations and tasks, set priorities and adapt to changing conditions are absolutely critical. The skill is difficult to articulate at times because it has become so much a part of our everyday lives.

Adaptability is keeping calm and persisting in the face of difficulties while taking on new challenges on short notice. In today's fast-paced and ever-changing world, it's about bouncing back, improvising and keeping an open mind. Most importantly, it is about seeing the bigger picture.

Rarely in life do we get to make any of the rules; therefore, if you want to exist peacefully, you need to adapt. The more flexible you are, the more successful you will be. As my past would suggest, my success isn't necessarily based on my talent. Instead, it is a testament to how hard I have worked and adapted to change. In other words, my mindset has always been to work hard and not give up. When something doesn't go according to plan, my mind immediately cycles through all the ways I could make it work with the resources available. For many, the tendency is to focus negatively on the obstacle itself instead of looking for ways to overcome it. Rather than making excuses, learn to become more adaptable and flexible.

Have a Plan B. Before you take a trip that involves travel, do you have a contingency plan if your flight is canceled or is delayed? In the military, the adage is, "Expect the best, plan for the worst." Think through some alternative scenarios ahead of time so you won't be caught off guard and stressed out to the point of not thinking clearly.

In most situations, there is something you can control. Even if the only thing you can control is how you respond to others, at least you'll have that to lean on. My former secretary taught me many

STEP SO FAR OUT OF YOUR COMFORT ZONE THAT YOU FORGET HOW TO GET BACK.

things, but the one phrase I always remember is her saying, "You will never regret your silence." If you can commit to working hard on the things only you can control and accepting the situation, you will be better suited to adapt and change as things around you become chaotic. Adapting is about using your strengths rather than trying to be something you are not and unwillingly yielding rather than willfully adjusting.

One way to improve your adaptability is to deliberately put yourself in situations that make you uncomfortable. The common phrase is *getting outside your comfort zone.*

Maybe that explains why two sons can be raised in the same house, with the same parents, go to the same church, attend the same schools, hear the same instruction, grow up with the same neighbors, eat the same food – well, you get the gist – and yet turn out so differently. One son moves way outside his comfort zone, and while he remembers how to get back, he never looks back. Years later, his wife marvels at the difference between her husband and his brother. She also recognizes that her husband is more adaptable than her brother-in-law and finds it easier to go with the flow.

There is no guarantee that planning ahead, controlling what you can and getting out of your comfort zone will make you suddenly more adaptable. However, you will begin to find it easier to make the most of a bad situation. Your confinement will be directly related to the walls you build.

The next time you are hungry for a $50 steak and can't afford it, go to a fancy restaurant and order a $10 dessert instead. Oh, and be sure to ask for a cherry on top!

ADVENTURE

**IF WE WERE MEANT TO
STAY IN ONE PLACE, WE'D
HAVE ROOTS INSTEAD OF FEET.**

The term *adventure* is, in a sense, value-neutral. An adventure can be frightening, or it can be great. Yet, where would we be without a little adventure? As Eleanor Roosevelt once stated, "The purpose of life is to live it, to taste experience to the utmost, to reach out eagerly and without fear for a newer and richer experience." In other words, we grow and become our best selves when we take advantage of new adventures.

The definition of adventure is engaging in an unusual and exciting, typically hazardous, experience or activity. For most, adventure is about stepping out of your comfort zone and opening up to the experiences and beauty that life gives you, no matter what path you choose. Adventure is all about taking each experience, regardless of whether you know the outcome or not, and facing it head on. It's about seeing the world from a different perspective even if you've seen it a million times before. It is choosing to see beauty in the ordinary.

For Alise McGregor, adventure was transforming the traditional industry of daycare for children and focusing on learning instead of playing. While playing, sharing, conscientiousness and making friends were all part of her adventure, Alise aspired to provide an extensive educational foundation and skills that would benefit children for life. Today, Little Newtons, a multimillion-dollar daycare business in Minnesota, continues to grow and expand because more parents are realizing the importance of early childhood development.

Adventure does not always mean traveling to some exotic destination on your bucket list. It can be exploring something new and choosing to look at it differently. It can be taking a road trip not because you want to reach a particular destination, but because the journey will uncover surprises. I have always enjoyed vacationing in Myrtle Beach, South Carolina. I used to take my two sons as a

DARE TO DO SOMETHING OUT OF THE ORDINARY.

single father and now enjoy sharing the experience with my two sons, two stepsons, three daughters-in-law, five grandsons, two granddaughters and my wife. The difference today is that the entire trip is now an adventure instead of a vacation destination.

Adventure adds value in so many ways. My wife has introduced me to numerous cuisines and added color to my attire. Although I am the author of *Enjoy The Ride,* she is the one most often introducing us to new experiences – whether I like it or not. No one will ever accuse me of living in the safety of a comfort zone. At the end of my life, I trust people will have seen me as someone who seized opportunities and took on everything with passion, enthusiasm and excitement. Whether you are skydiving, caring for patients as a nurse or chasing your kids around your yard, choose to see every day as a miracle.

Life is a big adventure, and it's up to you to choose how you are going to live it. That choice will determine how much value you add to your own life and the lives of others. The most precarious risk of all is not doing what you want while betting you will be able to do it later. Maybe it's true that people care when it's too late. Don't wait until it's too late to tell someone how much you love and care about them. When they're gone, it's too late. Sometimes the words we leave unspoken are the most important ones.

So let's all put our cell phones, laptops and tablets down and stop looking for a remarkable adventure online. Yours can be as simple as befriending a random person at a coffee shop. Do something different every day, and you will live a life of adventure.

So what are you waiting for? Go out and claim your own adventure. Go add another cherry!

AMBITION

PURSUE SOMETHING THEY SAID YOU COULDN'T DO.

As a former sales and marketing manager, I always told our team that if you don't go after what you want, you'll never have it, and you will always get zero percent of what you don't ask for. I was mentored to surround myself with a character of people who have dreams, desires and ambitions because they would help me realize my own. Therefore, it is easy to see how ambition adds value.

Remember when George Jung (aka Johnny Depp) said, in *Blow*, "My ambition far exceeds my talents"? It was one of the most inspiring lines I ever heard in a movie. Ambition is what fuels our passion and allows us to pursue our goals with complete disregard of circumstances and outcomes. Those with this innate drive to succeed will see the end first, and it will justify the means. It's worth mentioning that ambition isn't a bad thing. It isn't greed or addiction to power.

Ambition is the desire to escape mediocrity, which, incidentally, is the place where too many people choose to live. Ambitious people understand that there are no shortcuts to fulfillment, contentment and living a meaningful life. They know that life is nothing short of hard work, and that in order to succeed you must do the heavy lifting.

Ambition is about pushing all your chips to the middle of the table and going all in. When I resigned as an executive at a greeting card company after an eleven-year career, I knew it was the only path that would get me closer toward my goal of speaking and writing. I have had plenty of highs, lows, ups and downs over my last twenty years as a professional speaker; however, I wouldn't trade all the pain and mistakes for all the gain. Prove your family, friends, neighbors and the world wrong. Master your craft and become one of the elite. Most people won't!

YOUR AMBITION WILL ALWAYS DRIVE YOU FORWARD.

In Webster's Dictionary, ambition is defined as "a strong drive for success." This drive is a common trait in anyone who has created major success or left a significant mark on the world. Anyone who has moved the world forward in any meaningful way has had ambition. Through sheer will and a burning ambition, Henry Ford created the most prominent car manufacturing empire in the world at the time and revolutionized the auto industry as well as manufacturing processes in general. It wasn't a Harvard education that got the job done; it was a burning desire put into action toward a vision.

We can easily assume that this kind of burning desire is not common, because we don't see it in everyday life. Now that we know how important ambition is if we genuinely want to succeed at any significant level, we need to understand how to utilize our ambition to get there.

In my experience, it requires having a vision or goal that greatly inspires us. The more important we make it, the more we are driven to create it. We must feed that vision regularly in order to get the job done.

Never forget that talent and genius are quite abundant – you can find creative and brilliant people all over the place. Truly ambitious visionaries, however, are a rare breed and usually define the future for everyone else.

Be on the edge. Live large, dream big and obsess about it until you make it real!

APPROACHABILITY

**PEOPLE WITH THE BUSIEST
SCHEDULES FIND THE TIME
TO HELP WHEN IT IS NEEDED.**

The word approachable derives from the Latin verb *appropriare,* which means "to come nearer to." The first thing to remember is that approachability is a two-way street. It's both you stepping onto someone else's front porch, and you inviting someone to step onto yours.

Being approachable is key to building relationships and adding value with your colleagues. When you're approachable, people have the confidence that you will not overreact when they bring issues to you. That makes them less likely to sit on or cover up problems.

Reserved parking spots, gatekeepers and other ivory tower markers make some leaders unapproachable. Often, these symbols are a way of maintaining authority. However, they are missing out on opportunities to identify issues or discover ideas for improvement by not being in touch with the front line. To be approachable, you have to reduce the power distance.

Approachability is about being accessible, breaking down barriers and communicating properly. The value of being approachable is priceless. What would happen if you wore a nametag that read "Hello, my name is Steve"? Would people be friendlier? Would people say hello and call you by name, or would they stare at you with a confused look on their face? The answer to all these questions and more is yes. The bottom line is that you have to want to be approachable. When you are, the opportunities that come your way will dramatically increase.

Not everyone has an outwardly magnetic force that attracts all types of people. Whether they're engaging you in a light and friendly chat or a meaningful conversation, they seem to have a presence you wish you had. Some people have it, and others don't, but that's a barren way of thinking about it. There's absolutely no reason why you can't also be the type of person who charms the pants off of everybody.

THE SECRET TO BECOMING APPROACHABLE AND LIKABLE IS SMILING.

In my preparation for this section, I asked a colleague I would consider being socially awkward, or just habitually shy, why it seemingly takes a lot of effort for them to have engaging interactions with others. They shared that if a person they are talking to seems uncomfortable, they start to think they have offended or bored them. A definite *aha* moment for me. What I learned through my colleague's transparency is that without some visible reassurance that communicates the person is listening and enjoying the conversation, you will struggle to be present and are bound to be forgotten.

Don't be that forgettable person. Learn the secret to magnetism and charm. Drum roll, please! Another drum roll, please! Guilty as written! A former CEO once asked me, "Steve, what is bothering you? In your position as an executive, people are already apprehensive to approach you. When you're not smiling, they are definitely not going to open up and give you their opinion." After that, I made a colossal effort to forge a bond with my subordinates by creating a positive first impression and always exercising welcoming body language, including using their name in our conversation, asking questions about them and most definitely smiling.

Research has always revealed that facial expressions influence our initial impression and convey qualities of warmth and competence. Be mindful of the fact that your facial expressions and body language will tell a person if you are approachable.

AUTHENTICITY

DON'T BE AFRAID OF BEING DIFFERENT; BE AFRAID OF BEING THE SAME AS EVERYONE ELSE.

Authenticity is about staying true to you. It can seemingly be impossible to be real in all situations. Think of your social, romantic and professional relationships and ask yourself, "Is this really me, or am I choosing what parts of me I share depending on the situation?" Chances are, if you are like most people, you tend to be a different version of yourself depending on the setting. We hide certain traits and quirks about ourselves to fit the people surrounding us. In a professional setting, we may tone down and be a lot more formal than we might be at a restaurant with close friends. We may also discover that we put on a different version of ourselves with different friends. We often mold ourselves and emphasize specific characteristics while hiding the other parts.

Authenticity is a term meaning real, genuine or credible. The opposite meaning is false, phony or dishonest. When attributed to adding value, it is somewhat complicated. When something can make a person think deeply and assign an essential meaning to it, look to a person's belief system and their sense of reality. What a person believes adds value may be merely artificial, which would disputably be a false sense of worth. For example, some people hold the belief that if they don't get the newest iPhone they will not be happy. Do you really need the new iPhone? Were these ideas grown from the mind organically, or did they come from a type of manipulation that constantly dictates what we should do to achieve a sense of false fulfillment? I suspect the latter. Not only are we influenced in such a way that we incessantly purchase things we don't particularly need to fill some sort of void we're told we have, we don't even realize we are being controlled. To make matters worse, it's not only applied to products like iPhones and the latest handbag trend, but it can also apply to worldwide views.

WHEN WE STAND BY WHAT WE TRULY BELIEVE IN, PUTTING OUR BELIEFS ABOVE OTHERS IS WHAT EARNS US RESPECT.

Authenticity adds value because without it how can there be any change and self-actualization? In history, change has come from people who refused to be manipulated and chose a path of bettering themselves and challenging the status quo.

It's not about going with the crowd; it's about being true to you. Sometimes you may not agree with the rest; therefore, you do not need to follow just to be liked by others. Respect is earned by being the person in the room that is so firm in his or her beliefs that they will not let the crowd sway their opinion. As a board member at a financial institution, one thing that has served me well was the advice of a fellow member who said, "Own your truths, stand up and stand out."

Remember, not every person is going to like you, but having faith that the real you is, in fact, awesome will make room for those people who absolutely adore the real you. It is so much easier when we don't have to worry about thinking about how we are acting, what we should be hiding and what we should be sharing.

When you find your true authenticity and allow it to be showcased all the time, you will begin to gain clarity and figure out what situations don't feel right. Start from a position of honesty with yourself and go from there. To become more authentic, become open-minded. We are inclined to attract the people and things we want in life when we're more receptive. This often leads to opportunities and new ways of thinking that expand our minds and bring us ideas that add value to our lives.

Authenticity offers a mixed message because it's now ever-present in business, blogs and periodicals. Everyone wants to be authentic. Unfortunately, the people who preach its value often don't understand its meaning. We're all looking for people who are honest, trustworthy and kind. It's time to add value and represent our true nature and beliefs.

BALANCE

STABILITY IS NOT SOMETHING YOU FIND. IT'S SOMETHING YOU CREATE.

Entrepreneurs are the absolute worst when it comes to having balance in their lives. I know because I am one. We think about business 24/7, and we become completely addicted to the action. We have such a passion for what we are doing that we lose sight of everything beyond work. We become so hyper-focused on getting things done that we forget to notice the incredibly beautiful world around us. The problem becomes that we get so engrossed in our work that we completely forget that having balance in life is a key ingredient for achieving success.

Balance is a feeling derived from being whole and complete. It's a sense of harmony, essential to maintaining quality in life and work. Your life is made up of many vital areas, including your health, family, career, finances, intellect, social work, spirituality, recreation, personal growth and romance. You won't necessarily spend time every day in each area in equal amounts, but if in the long run you spend a sufficient quantity and quality of time in each, your life will feel in balance. However, if you neglect any one area, not to mention two or three, you will eventually sabotage your success. Much like a table, if one leg is longer or shorter than the others, it'll become wobbly. For instance, if you don't take care of your health, your family and social life will suffer. If you put too much time into running your business, personal relationships and self-care may suffer.

Living a balanced life is about integrating those components that are truly important to you and realizing that sometimes you need to make choices about what has to come first. By choosing what comes first, sometimes there are sacrifices. But living a balanced life doesn't require you to give 100 percent of yourself 100 percent of the time. There will be times when family life and work collide, but by knowing what's most important to you and making choices accordingly, you'll be better able to balance your decisions and feel whole.

MAKING CHOICES IS POWERFUL AND ALLOWS YOU TO LIVE A BALANCED LIFE THAT'S ALIGNED WITH WHAT YOU VALUE.

For a lot of people, a healthy work-life balance seems like an impossible goal. With so many of us torn between juggling heavy workloads, managing relationships and family responsibilities, and squeezing in outside interests, it's no surprise that more than one in four American's describe themselves as stressed. In our rush to "get it all done" at the office and at home, it's easy to forget that as our stress levels spike, our productivity plummets. Stress can destroy our concentration, make us irritable or depressed, and harm our personal and professional relationships. Over time, stress also weakens our immune system and makes us susceptible to a variety of health issues, from catching a simple cold to doubling the risk of having a heart attack.

The key to managing stress is in that one magic word: balance. Not only is achieving a healthy work-life balance an attainable goal, but workers and businesses alike see the benefits. When workers are balanced and happy, they are more productive, take fewer sick days and stay in their jobs longer.

Years ago, I defined success only in the context of career and how far up the corporate ladder I could climb. Business and life experiences have taught me to develop a much broader perspective.

At the end of the day, this is all about living a regret-free existence. Later in life, you don't want to look back and feel bad about neglecting your children, your health or your career aspirations because you didn't take the steps necessary to make things better. Balance isn't easy to achieve, but it is well worth the effort. Make a commitment to add value to your life. Find that balance today!

CHARACTER

**CHARACTERIZE PEOPLE
BY THEIR ACTIONS,
AND THEIR WORDS WILL
NEVER FOOL YOU.**

Character is forged through adversity, developed through lived values and becomes the defining "characteristic" of your nature. Adversity is relative and based on how each of us perceives challenging or trying times. I would suggest that we look at the firefight as fun, and the bullets we dodge as part of the thrill necessary to accomplish our objective. I think one of our aims is to improve the lives of others by offering the lessons of our character. Character is the anchor of success.

One of the most critical measures of a person's character is how they treat people they will get nothing from in return. I am never shocked, but will always be baffled, that some people never outgrow the need to treat others differently based on their egocentricities. Most people are nice to the people who can help them. At some level, in some way, it is almost expected in this day and age. But how do people treat those who can do nothing to help them? Some are indifferent; others are anywhere from haughty to hostile. How you handle the clerk at the checkout counter compared to your neighbor with the barking dog says a lot about your character.

Perhaps the most important mental and spiritual principle ever discovered is that what is going on outside of you is a reflection of what is going on inside of you. You can tell the inner condition and character of a person by looking at the outer conditions of his or her life. Your mind is extraordinarily powerful. Your thoughts control and determine almost everything that happens to you. They can make you happy or sad, sometimes in an instant. They can make you popular or unpopular, confident or insecure, positive or negative.

How a person plays "the game" reveals part of his or her character; however, how he or she loses reveals it all. As a matter of fact, how a person reacts to any emotional situation will explain a little bit about their character. This includes love, loss, remorse, anger, stress,

WHAT YOU THINK,

YOU ARE –

NOT WHAT YOU

THINK

YOU ARE.

sadness and so many other things. More times than not, when an inconvenience develops, and we are faced with a chance to grow and add value to our life or to the lives of others, we take a nose-dive because we lack the necessary character.

Another test of a person's character is how they handle power. Imagine you're escorted to an office. You sit down and learn that you and a partner need to complete ten tasks. Since your partner is running late, it's up to you to pick five tasks for yourself. You get to delegate the other five tasks to your partner. Some of the tasks are very short; others will require much more time. Will you act like a taker, claiming the short tasks for yourself and leaving your partner stuck with the long ones? Or will you be a giver, doing the time-consuming work and letting your partner off the hook? Your reputation is what other people think you are. Your character is what you really are. You want your reputation and your character to match, but concentrate on your character. You may be able to fool others about the kind of person you really are for a time, but it seldom lasts for long. The surest way to make sure your character and your reputation are the same is to live in such a way that nothing you do would embarrass you if it were printed on the front page of the newspaper. Good character means never taking ethical shortcuts even though everyone else may be doing so. You build good character by doing the right thing because it's the right thing to do. You add value to yourself and others by having good character.

CHARISMA

APPEAL IS INVISIBLE ENERGY WITH VISIBLE EFFECTS.

Charisma is a magnetic energy that expresses confidence and elicits admiration from others. Some people are born with natural charisma and an outgoing personality that magnetically attracts others to them; however, you don't necessarily have to be born with charisma. The good news is that it can be acquired over time, yet it only manifests in the company of others. You have to cultivate a reputation for being informed and interesting.

Charisma adds value because it will help win people over to your way of thinking. Similarly, it will help you in your livelihood and improve friendships because of your capacity to impact people with your words and actions. Having a charismatic personality will open doors of opportunity as you build trust and win the respect of those around you.

Confidence and charisma are in some ways joined at the hip. Failure is imminent if you lack the confidence, conviction and belief in your own abilities. When it comes to your social interactions with others, it is unequivocally vital that you first work on developing your confidence before anything else. However, it is also essential that you develop the necessary conviction and belief in your opinions and ideas. You will seldom gain the respect of others if you lack conviction.

To acquire a charismatic personality, grow your mindset in ways that will yield an attitude that fosters it. Here are some ways you can develop a charismatic mindset:

- Be *humble*. Humility will help you to keep your feet on the ground no matter how much loyalty you garner from others.

- Be *optimistic*. Optimism will help you to stay positive during difficult times.

- Be *passionate*. A charismatic individual is passionate, purpose-driven and enthusiastic about life.

THE EPICENTER OF CHARISMA IS AN ATTITUDE YOU HAVE ABOUT LIFE THAT YOU CONTINUALLY SHARE WITH OTHER PEOPLE THROUGH YOUR INTERACTIONS.

- Be *curious*. Curiosity will help you become more interested in other people's lives.

- Be *unpredictable*. Create a sense of intrigue about your persona to keep people guessing.

- Be *bold*. Have your own goals and vision, a sense of purpose, and create your own path, regardless of what obstacles stand in your way.

- Be *approachable*. A warm personality is friendly and outgoing and makes you very accessible.

- Be *grateful*. An abundance mentality means there is no deficiency in your life. You are grateful for everything.

Conversely, charisma isn't only about what you do, but rather also about what you avoid doing that could potentially ruin your reputation.

Here are a few things to avoid when developing a charismatic mindset:

- Don't *curse, gossip or complain*. It doesn't sound good, and it certainly won't do you any good either.

- Don't *talk excessively about yourself*. Focus the conversation instead on the other person's passions, problems and interests.

- Don't *attempt to please everyone*. It's impossible, and in the process, you might end up pleasing no one.

- Don't *interrupt people while they are talking*. This is one of the fastest ways to lose rapport.

- Don't *be arrogant*. Make people feel comfortable and at ease no matter how much their circumstances differ.

- Don't *make excuses*. Take responsibility for your life. Nobody wants to associate with those who explain their life away.

- Don't *lose control of your emotions*. Learn to control your emotions during troubled times, and it will help you gain incredible respect.

- Don't *take everything so seriously*. Have a playful and fun-loving nature. Find the humor in every difficulty, and help others feel at ease.

The steps you take to develop charisma may go against your persona; however, a whole new world of opportunity will open up to you as you begin winning the respect and admiration of those around you.

COMMON SENSE

**ONE POUND OF LEARNING
REQUIRES TEN POUNDS OF
COMMON SENSE TO APPLY IT.**

Growing up, my mom taught me common sense by example. She would say, "Now, does that make any sense? Think about it. Use some common sense." Other than the good Lord, she valued nothing more than common sense. Colleges now teach this with classes on "critical thinking," but too many young people fail to truly understand that many of life's problems can be fixed with common sense.

According to Wikipedia, common sense is sound practical judgment concerning everyday matters, or a basic ability to perceive, understand and judge that is shared by ("common to") nearly all people. The first type of common sense, good sense, can be described as "the knack for seeing things as they are and doing things as they ought to be done." The second type is sometimes described as folk wisdom, "signifying unreflective knowledge not reliant on specialized training or deliberative thought." The two types are intertwined as the person who has common sense is in touch with common-sense ideas, which emerge from the lived experiences of those commonsensical enough to perceive them.

But what is common sense? For me, it is not a simple thought process or ability. My common sense tells me that it is as complex as the factors inherent in any situation to which it might be applied. It is how we deal with issues and problems, how we manage our own thoughts, beliefs and attitudes, and how we cope with other people. It is essentially practical, not intellectual or academic. Common sense requires us to be flexible and ready to jettison habits and old ways of thinking when they do not serve us practically. This is one reason the practice of doing something different improves common sense.

Common sense is defined as good sense and sound judgment in practical matters. Through the years, I have met some smart and successful people with no common sense. Some of the emails I receive

> # COMMON SENSE IS A PRACTICAL VIEW AND APPROACH TO OURSELVES, TO OTHER PEOPLE AND TO ALL ASPECTS OF LIVING.

require me to respond with a healthy dose of common sense. I have improved my common sense by implementing these common-sense strategies:

- I remove myself from the situation to make a better decision.
- I don't overcomplicate things.
- I trust myself.
- I listen to myself.
- I divorce myself from my reality.
- I am okay being wrong.

You are not born with common sense – it simply manifests itself as you grow up. You learn what culture considers sound judgment and behave accordingly. This is nowhere near as obvious and easy as it seems to the more levelheaded people in our society. I would go so far as to say that if you don't have plenty of common sense by the time you're a teenager, and after getting burned repeatedly, you're never going to have it.

However, no two people are the same, and we all have a different way of doing things. We all have different priorities and biases that influence the very nature of how we tend to the things within our lives. It's only through sharing common experiences with common lessons, and in sharing common intellect with a common emotional intelligence, that we can all share a common sense – which is rare, if not altogether impossible.

When we believe someone lacks common sense, it's usually out of irritation from him or her not doing something exactly as we would have done it ourselves. In essence, we are expecting everyone to think, look and behave exactly as we do. We lack compassion for their circumstances, and we lack understanding for the differences between us.

We all have little hiccups in our thinking that sometimes distract us, and we get lost in thought. That is a common, shared human experience. We're not all mindful of the same things in the exact same moment, so step back and be more compassionate and less judgmental. Rid yourself of the burden of constantly comparing your behaviors to others assuming they will act like you. Use common sense. The world would be a better place if only common sense was more common.

COMMUNICATION

**IF YOU CAN'T EXPLAIN IT TO
A SIX-YEAR-OLD, YOU DON'T
UNDERSTAND IT YOURSELF.**

ccording to a University of Texas at Austin study, we speak on average approximately 16,000 words a day. Yet, we still don't use these words effectively. In a world of cell phones, texting, tweeting and emails, the need for effective communication has never been stronger than it is today because many can barely remember what verbal communication actually is, let alone how to execute it correctly. While it is important to be able to communicate well through our devices, we should remember how to speak properly if we want to add value and survive.

If you have ever watched *The Bachelorette*, you'll observe that the guys who make it furthest are the ones who get to spend the most time talking with the woman. This is because building a rapport with someone comes from talking and listening. When you can get to know each other and discover similarities, your relationship can build a more solid foundation. This applies to anything in life, such as clients and friendships.

Communication is the root of all events, daily interaction, social affairs and anything that requires human encounters. We have the technology to enhance communication by making it simpler, faster, effective and convenient no matter where you are on the globe. From its humble beginnings with handwritten letters delivered by men on horseback, to building virtual bridges between nations, we are continually adding value by communicating.

Developing communication skills can help many aspects of your life, from your professional career to social gatherings to your family life. In today's hectic world, we rely heavily on sharing information, resulting in greater emphasis being placed on having good communication skills. Good verbal and written communication skills are essential in order to deliver and understand information quickly and accurately. Being able to communicate effectively is a vital life skill and should not be overlooked.

COMMUNICATION IS KEY TO YOUR SUCCESS IN RELATIONSHIPS, IN THE WORKPLACE, AS A CITIZEN OF YOUR COUNTRY AND ACROSS YOUR LIFETIME.

In this day and age, smartphones have caused people to enter a whole new world. They force us to be antisocial, lose patience quickly, use incorrect spelling and grammar, and limit our face-to-face interactions with one another. Since texting and social media are now our primary forms of communication, people have begun to use abbreviations. This eases our ways of communication when sending a quick text to a friend, but a problem occurs when we are no longer texting, and we are now typing an important document.

Children are not practicing the proper skills they are going to need in the real world, which could lead to having a significant adverse effect in their future. Whereas, cell phones may add value to our lives, there are also many negative drawbacks. We need to change our ways of communication while we still can.

Clear communication is not easy. The method, context, structure, language, knowledge and understanding of the needs of the recipients to whom the information is being transmitted are vital. You want to make a good impression on your friends, family, instructors and employers. They all want you to convey a positive image, as it reflects on them. In your career, you will represent your business or company in spoken and written form. Your professionalism and attention to detail will reflect positively on you and set you up for success.

In today's world of instant communication, we often don't value the importance of communication skills that much. Highly effective people in business and personal relationships inherently understand the importance of communication skills, which is why some people enjoy success while others continually encounter difficulties expressing themselves and understanding others without generating conflict, misunderstandings and mistrust. Today's devices capture too much of our attention and cause us to shortchange personal conversations while we worry about our virtual relationships.

It's time to understand the importance of communication and become the effective communicators that we desire to be – and need to be.

COMPOSURE

WHEN YOU CAN'T CONTROL WHAT'S HAPPENING, CONTROL THE WAY YOU RESPOND TO IT.

Getting emotional is acceptable; however, there is a time and a place for emotion. I am not suggesting we go through life like a machine, because that isn't healthy. Nonetheless, in our pursuit to think clearly and objectively, we can't let our behavior and emotion hijack our actions.

The challenge with staying composed is that people read verbal and nonverbal cues from you and make judgments. That's what we all do. While we shouldn't care about how people judge us, the truth is we do. If people know there are buttons they can press that will rile you up and force you to lose composure, it becomes a weakness they can exploit. Remaining calm, cool and collected in all situations is a powerful tool. Composure shows self-confidence. You are sure of yourself, and you dictate your reality. External factors don't shake that.

We've all lost our composure at some point. When we lose composure, we let that excess emotion affect our behavior and actions, just like a child does. You've all seen the tiny tears when children don't get their way. Maybe you had a childhood friend who used to sulk and cry when he or she didn't win playing a video game. Perhaps that was you. When we're young, we have an idea of "normality," and we don't know how to properly deal with things that upset our understanding of the world. That's fine. We learn. Or do we? The key is becoming experienced in dealing with these things, feeling the frustration, the anger and the joy, and learning how to react without letting it mess with the logical part of our brains.

The good news is there are ways and means to help you keep your composure and add value to your life. First and foremost, don't take anything personally. It's tough. Someone says something against your beliefs to the point where you want to tell him or her they're wrong. Remember, everyone has a perspective. Everyone has a job to

DIFFERENT OPINIONS ARE WHAT MAKE THE WORLD SO DIVERSE.

do. Most of the time someone's perspective will not align with yours. Let's not forget an ordinary disregarded principle: *to each their own*.

When you're emotional, impulse isn't always the best way. Think before you act. Before you do anything, breathe and pause for a few seconds. Break the routine. If someone or something has irritated you, go for a walk. Go outside. Get some fresh air or change the scenery. Think it over. Relax. Let your emotions simmer so you can collect yourself. Think about what you want to accomplish at that moment. Do you want to blow this situation out of proportion, or do you want to diffuse it? A quiet moment to yourself gives you a chance to fully analyze things and make better decisions. Then make your choice and live with it.

When you do lose composure, learn from it. Identify what took your composure and ask yourself what you can do to stop it from happening again. Reflecting on why it happened and finding the purpose will make you start practicing self-awareness. What is the goal? When you complain, argue and battle with family, friends and strangers, it doesn't help you achieve your goals or better your life. If losing composure adds unnecessary stress, causes problems or influences you to lose sight of what's important, then what value is it adding?

You have a choice. You are the center of your world. When external factors wash against you, remain strong. You are the anchor. Bad things will happen, and your composure will be tested many times; however, you can choose how to react. You can define yourself on your terms. So the next time you feel yourself getting all hot and bothered, or your bottom lip starts quivering when things don't go your way, think about how much value composure will add to your life. Composure is a beautiful but fragile thing. Keep it and cherish it.

CONFIDENCE

BEING UNSURE OF YOURSELF MAKES IT DIFFICULT TO CONVINCE OTHERS TO BELIEVE IN YOU.

When I speak of confidence, I am not talking about blind arrogance. Overly confident people fall into yet another category. However, I am referring to the self-confidence needed to believe in one's skills, goals and ability to succeed. When you believe in yourself, you are more likely to take action, seize the moment and persevere long after those who doubt themselves.

Self-confidence is one's ability to judge his or her own social and personal standing with respect to his or her environment and be able to derive satisfaction out of it. Upbringing, work environment and levels of dedication toward pursuing a cause influence self-confidence. High self-confidence is an important factor in improving business ties and balancing personal life. An old adage says that when you start the journey of your professional life, have confidence in your abilities because you have not proven them yet. Right from the early times through the evolution of human society, this saying couldn't be truer in the context of the present. We live in extremely competitive times, and self-confidence is one of the most prominent pillars of strength for all of us.

To achieve even the smallest of goals, and to get through life's daily duties and responsibilities, self-confidence is a must. Developing a self-confident attitude allows you to wade through the push and pull of different voices and opinions telling you "yes, no, maybe, do this, do that." Relying on other people to guide you and following their opinions robs you of your individuality. Self-confidence is an attitude you hold about yourself that allows you to move forward and achieve your goals. Becoming self-confident does not mean you are unrealistic about yourself and your situation. You understand that you are not super-human, but being confident means still moving toward your desires even when things don't seem to be going your way.

SELF-CONFIDENCE IS KNOWING YOU ARE GOOD, WORTHY AND CAPABLE OF FACING LIFE'S DIFFICULTIES.

Not everyone knows how important self-confidence is. It can change your whole life for the better, while a lack of confidence will have an adverse effect on your social relations, career, achievements and even your mood. Self-confidence and happiness are strongly connected.

Now, why would a person who feels that way experience bad emotions? Actually, the moments when we feel bad the most are when our self-confidence is at its lowest point. In other words, the more confident you become, the happier you will be. When we know and appreciate who we are, we feel great about ourselves. We make better choices and decisions, creating a better life for ourselves.

This is extremely important in every aspect of our lives, yet so many people struggle to find it. It's a worldwide problem for people of all ages, genders and races. Our confidence is perfectly intact when we are born, but diminishes during our childhood. We lose a little of it when we make mistakes, fail, misbehave, get in trouble, feel guilty, neglect ourselves and do things we are ashamed of. As we all know, children can be mean. Many of us can relate to being bullied or picked on as children, which can destroy our confidence, too. Your confidence is not controlled by anyone else, however. You have absolute control and can become confident anytime in your life, regardless of past experiences.

Building your confidence is like exercising a muscle. It relies on small, incremental improvements on a daily basis. You don't acquire perfect tone for life in a single hour. So, regular confidence building is the only way to lasting confidence and happiness. With dedication and determination, you can learn to love and trust yourself unconditionally. Everything in your life changes for the better once you do, and that, my friend, adds value!

CONSISTENCY

**WHAT YOU DO EVERY DAY
MATTERS MORE THAN WHAT
YOU DO EVERY ONCE IN A WHILE.**

Consistency is as important as truth. How can you ever be true to your word if your actions are continually unpredictable? Inconsistency is characteristically unclear and can cause people to believe you have an ulterior motive. This is a factor in both personal and professional relationships.

Consistency is important because it expresses who you are and what character you have. It shows people you mean business. If you are having trouble succeeding in life, look at what you do every day. Are you always complaining and/or snapping at people when they say something to you? Are you frequently late? When you recognize your negative behaviors, you will either ignore them or commit to change. We have the ability to replace bad habits with new ones. Be consistent in your kindness, love and patience, and you will start seeing the change. Start small so you don't overwhelm yourself. Being consistent is not giving up at the first sign of trouble.

In February 2015, I made the decision to start writing a blog and committed to writing one a week. When I started, I questioned myself and wasn't entirely convinced I would stick to it. The funny thing about expectations is you usually end up getting what you expect. I ended the year writing nine blogs. Disgruntled with my lack of consistency, I soon realized that writing a weekly blog was not a single act, but rather a daily habit. The ultimate element would be to write a little every day. Whether you want to write a blog, write a book or lose weight, the key is consistency. In 2016, I ended the year by writing 57 blogs that contained over 45,000 words. Now I write three blogs every month and a feature article for my newsletter. In my spare time, I wrote this book. Consistency creates momentum and is a habit you can learn. Surprisingly, doing something every day, or almost every day, is far easier than doing it once in a while.

What is that one thing you want to do more consistently? Stop waiting for the conditions to be right and desirable. Conditions are

THERE IS NO 100% CONSISTENCY!

rarely suitable, and you can count on failure at some stage. However, if you use the failure as a means to capture feedback and improve, then getting back on track will be easier. Choose the task you want to focus on and promise yourself you will accomplish it by taking small steps. Stand firm despite the lows and keep pushing toward the goal. If you're going after 100% consistency and beating yourself up every time you get off track, you're setting yourself up for failure. No human being is consistent 100% of the time. If you do venture off course, that's okay. Get back on track, learn from it and focus on being more consistent moving forward.

As I have stated numerous times in my writings, when you make a shift in your mindset, it shifts everything and becomes a permanent, lasting change. For me, writing, reading, drinking my first cup of coffee with my wife (when I am home), brushing my teeth, not watching the news and eating healthy are all habits. These are all actions I do every single day of my life without even needing to think about them very much. They're automatic.

To be more consistent, begin to associate pleasure with the things you do. I'm always thinking about the pleasure and the benefits I get from doing the above-mentioned things. When I think about the satisfaction I get from receiving an email from someone who enjoyed my blog or book, it motivates me to be consistent. If I linked pain to writing, it wouldn't be long before I would need a lot of willpower to sit down and create. A compliment on how good you look and a renewed energy when walking up a flight of stairs will make eating healthy much easier. When you find a way to associate pleasure with various components of your life and align your daily habits to them, that's the description for consistency.

COOPERATION

**LOOK FOR THE BEST WAY INSTEAD
OF INSISTING ON YOUR WAY.**

Cooperation exists at many levels and takes place between individuals and organizations as well as between governments. Cooperation allows participants to exchange valuable information that helps both sides improve their knowledge bases and work in an efficient manner. Cooperation involves working hand in hand for everyone's benefit. Whether it is applied at home, at work or in social settings, cooperation leads to achieving goals in better and more efficient ways.

No one has to lose for you to win, and yet we see just the opposite in so many organizations. Is everyone working together? If you buy a pit bull and a Labrador retriever, and one bites your leg off while the other brings it back to you, that may be working together, but it's not beneficial. Success depends on creating interpersonal relationships where everything is connected and everyone takes responsibility for positive results. Cooperation means helping each other out. In healthy teams, you don't hear comments such as "That's not my job" or "That's above my pay grade."

To encourage cooperation, compete with yourself against your past performance. If you regularly strive to outperform yourself, others will support you. This type of competitive cooperation promotes mutual inspiration. It allows people and groups to work together to achieve a common goal or to derive mutual benefit.

Cooperation is a basic process of social life. Society cannot exist without it. Human survival can only be accomplished if human beings collaborate and work together in the pursuit of common goals or common interests. It implies regard for the wishes of others and involves sacrifice, effort, reduction of private interests and an emphasis on community. You can accomplish things no one person could manage alone. Rearing, caring for, teaching and protection of a child are almost impossible without the help of others. Skills are

TO LIVE IN HARMONY, LEARN TO AGREE TO DISAGREE WITHOUT LETTING LITTLE THINGS DIVIDE YOU.

acquired, knowledge is accumulated, and methods are developed and passed on to the next generation.

Mutual self-interest is the real driver of cooperation. Sometimes we forget that the other person is making an equally large allowance for us. However, sometimes you have to agree to disagree when you believe their opinion is not based on fact, but rather their deep-seated selfishness. Give and take doesn't mean they give and you take. It means everyone must compromise, which sometimes can be problematic. A bad agreement is where everyone feels taken advantage of; whereas, a good compromise is where everyone thinks they conceded only a little. When you can only see and do things your way you miss so many opportunities to grow beyond your self-seeking notion.

No individual has adequate experience, education and knowledge to guarantee success without the cooperation of others. Not until you believe that nobody can get there unless everybody gets there will you ever fully see the value in cooperation. We now live in a more multifaceted world, where cooperating with others is essential to accomplishing something. To align yourself with other people who can add value to what you are doing requires you to be humble and genuine. Today's political arena looks like a battlefield of discord instead of a playing field with teammates making contributions. The competitive landscape is destroying feelings of cooperation. Accomplishment and proficiency are being surrendered and replaced with personal ambition and fear of rejection. Cooperate with others and compete with yourself. You will learn more, grow more and add more value.

COURAGE

YOU NEVER KNOW HOW STRONG YOU ARE UNTIL BEING STRONG IS THE ONLY CHOICE YOU HAVE.

Real courage requires wisdom. Everyone is afraid of something or someone. The difference is how you deal with your fear. Courage is something that everybody wants because it is an element of good character that makes us worthy of respect. We all have heard stories about courage. From the Bible to fairy tales, and ancient myths to Hollywood movies, our culture is rich with exemplary tales of bravery. From the cowardly lion in *The Wizard of Oz* to *Harry Potter*, children are raised on a diet of heroic and inspirational tales.

However, we all too often equate courage to physical bravery. What about social activists such as Martin Luther King Jr. and Nelson Mandela, who chose to speak out against injustice at significant personal risk? Entrepreneurs such as Steve Jobs and Walt Disney, who took financial risks to follow their dreams, are modern-day knights, exemplifying the rewards that courage can bring. Courage ranges from physical strength and endurance to mental stamina and innovation.

The first step to being courageous is to define your personal values and beliefs and live by them. Everyone has an opinion, which means there is a tremendous amount of opportunity to be sidetracked from your voice. Defining your truth requires you to be honest about what drives you, what you believe and what you fear. Even people we view as extremely strong in mind and body have been fearful. To conquer fear, face it. Use fear as a motivator to achieve your goals.

Twenty years ago, I walked away from a remarkable career and a good company. I was well compensated and received numerous accolades for my work. Within a month after leaving corporate America, someone told me they thought I was very brave for my decision. I dismissed the comment back then, believing that courage meant overcoming extraordinary challenges. Not until a few years later did it occur to me that I demonstrated bravery every day. As an entrepreneur whose entire income, health benefits and lifestyle

YOU CAN TURN FEAR INTO AN ASSET RATHER THAN AN OBSTACLE DEPENDING ON HOW YOU USE IT.

depended on me accomplishing my goals, I was dealing with a variety of obstacles and a multitude of fears as part of my daily life. For the most part, we dismiss our ability to overcome fear because it never appears worthy of acknowledgment. How many times as a child did you not raise your hand and respond to a question because of fear? Years later, you sit in a meeting that is dominated by other people's opinions and struggle to share yours.

It takes courage to step out of your comfort zone. We are so convinced our opinion will be dismissed that it takes tremendous resolve to share our point of view. While you want to make sure you don't talk just to talk, you do need to challenge the status quo when appropriate. It takes courage to offer different ideas to stimulate new thinking in other people. When you positively present your ideas, they can't label you a naysayer. From my experience, when you unlock the current thinking of your team, you emerge as a leader.

The real challenge is to eliminate the "what-ifs" from your thinking – *What if I'm wrong? What if they laugh at me?* "What-ifs" give fear too much power. Instead, use fear as the stimulus to grow and become stronger, more resilient.

The truth is that we need courage every day, not just in extreme circumstances. We need the courage to be a good mother or father, husband or wife, boss or employee. It requires changing habits, developing real confidence in ourselves and exerting self-control. So strengthen your heart and build your courage. Every day presents moments when you will need it.

CREATIVITY

THE WILLINGNESS TO DO SOMETHING THAT MAY NOT WORK CREATES ABUNDANCE OUT OF NOTHING.

In this fast-paced world, technology is changing rapidly, and everything adapts with the blink of an eye. So, if you want to go along with the world, then a primary requirement is to be creative. Now, before you proclaim you're not a creative person, go back to the table of contents, and you will discover that there isn't a chapter on imagination. The reason is that creativity relies on you using your imagination as the process to generate new ideas, alternatives, solutions and possibilities.

Creativity is the ability to conceive something unpredictable, original and unique. It is the mirror of how beautifully a person can think in any given circumstance. It is not genetic, but can be developed if you keep learning and comprehending things while exploring the perceptions of others. When you brainstorm and use your imagination, it is amazing how many times you unveil something that was previously hidden.

In school, those who could write a good story or draw beautiful pictures are considered creative, but research shows that all people are. Creativity is one of the most fundamental characteristics of being human. All too often, a creative idea is defined as one that is both novel and useful in a particular setting. We see creativity as reserved for IT, science, math, writing, art or theater. So why aren't we all more creative? Rules and regulations often stifle us. Our school systems typically disapprove of imagination, daydreaming and imperfection. Revolutionary ideas come from people who genuinely are self-described daydreamers. Educational systems all too often teach us not to think differently, but to follow instructions and obey the status quo. Creativity is no longer just seen as what artists and musicians process, however. It is a skill for professionals in all fields.

The benefits of creativity are nearly endless. Here are several reasons why it adds value:

CREATIVITY INSPIRES HAPPINESS AND A DESIRE TO SHARE THAT WITH OTHERS.

Widespread – It isn't limited to a certain person or job. Not only can you practice creativity through many different mediums, but its benefits also apply to almost all professions.

Self-Discovery – I have observed that when my employees learn more about who they are and recognize how that fits into our business, they share a hidden side of themselves. I've heard them say, "I guess I never knew I was creative."

Problem-solving – When you approach a problem from an array of angles instead of the conventional way, you usually uncover a better solution.

Well-being – Our company meetings encourage all ideas and have a playful approach. We try to promote a sense of joy and security without the fear of feeling inadequate.

Focus – Creativity is more about dedication and commitment. Imagination essentially improves your ability to concentrate and explore.

Self-confidence – Writing a book isn't easy; writing a book people will read and appreciate is even harder. Creativity requires courage, confidence and the willingness to write twenty pages, throw them away and write twenty more.

Innovation – Every advancement known to humanity started with a new idea, and new ideas are inspired by imagination and creativity.

Humility – There is always room for improvement, and creativity requires humbleness to challenge your ideas until new growth occurs.

Creativity makes life infinitely exciting and fulfilling. It is a way of living life that embraces originality and makes unique connections between seemingly contrasting ideas. Creativity is about living life as a journey into seeing and communicating the surprising and plainest acts of everyday life. It's about painting your masterpiece, on your canvas, and creating abundance out of nothing.

DETERMINATION

**EVERYBODY WANTS TO BE A
DIAMOND, BUT VERY FEW ARE
WILLING TO GET CUT.**

People who lack determination want to achieve something, but they haven't figured out how to get out of the way of themselves. They often complain a lot, offer excuses and rarely tackle their weaknesses. Moreover, a person who lacks determination is not clear on their goals.

Set one goal, then create a path to achieve it. Your every action should be oriented toward that same goal. Keep your mindset positive and be determined even when you face failures. Determination comes with practice and can transform your life as well as the people around you.

Determination increases your chances of being successful at a particular task or achieving a particular goal. It can also help you to stay motivated, in control and continuing along your path in life when times are tough. Remember what gives you that determination to keep going so you can summon it when you encounter adversity or a challenging situation. The reason I've been unwavering despite countless setbacks and obstacles that have appeared throughout my journey is that I remember what makes me determined to keep going. For me, it has always been that opportunity to influence people's lives for the better and see a transformation happen in front of my own eyes.

The true definition of determination is the burning desire to accomplish something and not allowing anyone or anything to stop you. Without determination, you might give up in the face of difficulty or because naysayers put you down. Determined people have a lot of faith in their capacity to succeed. They focus on what they have rather than on what they don't have and exhibit gratitude. They are realistically optimistic. They accept their present circumstances and make the best of it.

How can we strengthen our resolve? Practice. Rinse. Repeat. The more you stick to it, the more you will do it. It is that simple, which

EMBRACING DOUBTS ABOUT YOUR ABILITY TO REACH YOUR GOALS WILL DISTORT YOUR DETERMINATION.

can be that hard. Stay determined in the little things, and you will gain momentum through all aspects of your life. Crossing something off your list makes you feel good and affirms that you are on the right path. Life is never smooth. In order to march fearlessly ahead, remind yourself of the small wins. Stop rushing! Steadily persist and exercise patience while you wait for results. Don't be discouraged, and never give up. Have faith and courage.

Adding value to your life is a process of selection and elimination or choosing between worthy and the worthless. You will be hard-pressed to find many people in the world who flourished without an unremitting fight to reach their goals. Therefore, nothing is more important than our mental attitude. Miseries are common in every life cycle, and worries are persistent visitors. It isn't unusual to worry a little and be overcome with the lure to quit. As a matter of fact, quitting is a natural reaction to resistance and all too often the chosen response. The individual who stands against adversity and refuses to quit accomplishes so much more.

Determination comes down to personality. Those who are very strong, disciplined and determined are more likely to succeed in life. You can't be overwhelmed by the challenges and circumstances that come your way. Quitting is not an option, and failing to reach a goal is not an invitation to give up on it and set a different one instead. While it may sound good to have an alternative path to take, escape can become a bad habit. If you want to achieve goals in your life, learn how to embrace failure and perceive it as a lesson that gets you closer to succeeding. Remain steadfast and not easily overwhelmed by failure. Determination allows you to cross the finish line and make your dreams come true.

DISCIPLINE

**THE MASTERY OF LIFE IS
THE MASTERY OF SELF.**

Too many people are susceptible to instant gratification. People lacking control are unable to see the long-term results of their actions, which validates why discipline adds so much value. As the bridge between goals and accomplishment, it's probably the most crucial factor when trying to achieve a goal. Discipline can be developed or strengthened at any given time if you put your mind to it. It's a concept everyone is aware of, but few truly understand. The most successful people in life exercise discipline on a daily basis. It's vital to every living being, and without it, the world around us would be chaos. Discipline brings structure and teaches responsibility.

Whether at home, work or school, discipline plays an essential role in many aspects of life. Important to learn at a young age, it teaches us that there are consequences associated with poor behavior such as having altercations with other people. Having discipline also shows respect and consideration for others, which are valuable assets in the professional world. In fact, discipline is considered to be fundamental for personal achievement, business success, government interaction and international relations.

In addition to work and professional life, discipline plays an essential role in people's private lives. Individuals who are disciplined are more likely to exhibit healthy eating habits and usually have more regular sleep and wake cycles. The result is that they become more motivated and inspired to do their best, which translates directly to success in the professional world and elsewhere. People who are disciplined often teach others to behave in the same way, which in turn produces a happier and healthier culture.

The most valuable form of discipline is self-imposed. Don't wait for things to regress so drastically that someone else must impose discipline in your life. For every disciplined effort, there are multiple rewards. Learn the discipline of sending a thank-you note. Learn the

YOUR LIFE IS GOING TO SERVE AS EITHER A WARNING OR AN EXAMPLE – A WARNING OF THE CONSEQUENCES OF A LACK OF AMBITION OR AN EXAMPLE OF TALENT PUT TO USE.

discipline of paying your bills on time, arriving at appointments on time or just using your time more effectively. Paying attention takes discipline. Learn to go to bed so you can wake up early. Learn all you can learn so you can teach all you can teach. Read more.

For most of us, discipline is a work in progress wrapped in good intentions. Discipline is a practice. Not every day will be perfect, but each day is progress. Self-imposed discipline is the ability to do what you should be doing, which often means putting off your immediate comfort or wishes in favor of long-term success. If you want to get back in shape, getting up at 5:00am is short-term discomfort; however, the long-term benefits are more energy and vitality. The problem is that most people are where they *want* to be instead of where they *need* to be. Discipline gives us the ability to push ourselves to get ahead.

One of the best methods for building self-discipline is to simply get started. More often than not, the hardest part of doing something you do not want to do is gaining momentum. It may seem like a daunting task, but force yourself to take action. It will feel uneasy at first, and you may want to quit, but once you build momentum, you will feel the flow. Writing this book, for example, is a formidable undertaking. It takes discipline, and momentum is vital. Knowing you are now reading it, though, is the long-term reward for me – and the inspiration I need to finish this chapter.

Stop and think of the last time you were disciplined and pushed yourself to do something you didn't want to do. How did you feel about yourself? The reason you felt proud is because each time you employ the discipline to do what you know you should be doing, you add value to your life and others.

ENTHUSIASM

**PASSION IS THE FUEL
THAT DRIVES PURPOSE.**

Enthusiasm is the energy and inspiration you feel when you're obsessed with a desire to achieve something. In this lifetime, you will meet numerous people who are highly talented but fail miserably because of an indifferent attitude. In other words, they are talented, but they are not passionate enough about their goals to take the required action. Enthusiasm can be the driving force to overcome indifference. Whatever your talent is, you will not succeed if you don't honestly believe in your mission. Strong beliefs in your goals will create a burning desire within you that will act as a driving force. If you are enthusiastic, you will believe in yourself and your mission.

Being enthusiastic in today's negative and sarcastic world can be challenging, but it hardwires us to be unafraid about other aspects of our lives. You will face troubled relationships, tragedy, hurt and failure. Some people will make unwise decisions that directly affect you. Accidents will happen. When pain enters your life, it's easy to get discouraged and want to give up. Enthusiasm is the fire that keeps you going in the midst of affliction. Without it, you lose steam.

Enthusiasm is probably one of the most attractive qualities a person can have, enhancing your appeal in personal and professional relationships. It's also a wonderful quality to find in others. It tends to make all kinds of interactions more desirable and can fulfill more of the potential of any situation or experience. Being enthusiastic not only makes you more attractive, it also makes your words and messages much more powerful. When you are feeling enthusiastic, that feeling comes through your body language and voice tonality. Let's face it, those two parts make up over 90 percent of communication, and that, my friend, adds a lot of value.

When a company has a strong culture, employees enjoy being at work because they are motivated not only by factors such as money,

ENTHUSIASM IS THE FUEL THAT BRINGS ABOUT A SUCCESSFUL RESULT.

but natural factors as well. An example of an organization with a phenomenal culture is the world famous Pike Place Fish Market in Seattle. If you have been to the Pike Place Fish Market in the past twenty years, you undoubtedly know the unique energy and enthusiasm projected by employees every single day. From crew order calls to throwing fish with each other and with customers, owner John Yokoyama and his employees have built a set of ideals and norms that work for them.

One of my favorite quotes is, "Nothing great ever happened without enthusiasm." If you want to live a great life, you absolutely must possess enthusiasm for everything you do. The difference between success and failure is often small. Two people with virtually the same amount of skill and talent can differ vastly in the amount of success they achieve. The difference is enthusiasm! In many endeavors, you don't have to be ten times better than the next person to achieve great success, only slightly better. In the world of professional golf, less than half a stroke per round separates the top player from the fiftieth.

Enthusiasm is like a magnet. It attracts the right things and people, who in turn help create the appropriate conditions for a positive result. It enables you to take advantage of the opportunities as they present themselves.

While I am a raving fan of Daniel Goleman and his writings on emotional intelligence, I believe enthusiasm is the key to managing your emotions. Enthusiasm allows you to control the emotional climate of any given situation. Enthusiasm is a state of mind that inspires action and is the most contagious of emotions.

To be enthusiastic, act enthusiastically!

FAILURE

SOMETIMES IT TAKES A GOOD FALL TO REALLY KNOW WHERE YOU STAND.

Anyone who has ever succeeded at anything is probably well acquainted with failure because achievement usually takes more than one try. Almost everyone agrees that failure can inspire people to work harder to reach their goals. However, factors such as personality and core motivations can also affect this. Thomas Edison failed a thousand times before he invented the light bulb. J.K. Rowling was recently fired from her secretary job when she started writing her first Harry Potter novel, and then *Harry Potter and the Sorcerer's Stone* was rejected twelve times by various publishers. The more you fail and recover and improve, the better you become as a person.

Resilience is pivotal to any ultimate success. Hope, dreams and an active imagination despite serious challenges are why many people do so well. In my company, every time we try something and fail, we reevaluate and learn from our mistakes. Then we change our approach accordingly. Personally, I have never seen failing as a flaw, but rather as part of the blueprint necessary to succeed. Think about the practice of science. The most common outcome from any experiment is failure. Although I often step way out of the comfort zone of my inner circle of people, I have survived failure and gained invaluable knowledge while continuing to be unrelenting in my pursuit to progress.

So why do some of us not comprehend failure as something that adds value? Because defeat engenders insecurity and fear. Instead, we choose to play it safe by doing the same things day in and day out, making the same safe choices over and over again. Never attempting anything new reduces the possibility of failing, but robs us of the opportunity to succeed. Taking risks, surviving the battle and coming out the other side arms us with valuable experiences that will serve us later in life.

WHEN YOU FAIL AND THEN TRY TO UNDERSTAND THE PROCESSES, YOU GAIN PERSPECTIVE AND DEVELOP INSIGHT.

Failure develops personal growth. Every time I have failed once or repeatedly, I have grown and matured. Each time you fail, you learn something new about yourself, which hopefully will help you grow and improve. In doing so, you can begin your journey of self-discovery to reach your personal and professional goals. Challenge yourself by taking risks to yield possible rewards. If it's worth it, you will commit to it and covet it. Endurance is the key factor.

Not giving up is essential to the failing process. When we fail, many of us feel like throwing in the towel. That is something that can cross our minds, but we should avoid at all costs. One of the more rewarding parts of owning a family business is watching those who work with you finally understand the value of failing. I have witnessed the changes in our employees' attitudes when the prospect of failing doesn't seem so dire. When they stop dreading failure, but rather welcome it as part of their journey, it changes their outlook.

Failure isn't the end of the world. It is part of a learning process that affords you vast knowledge and experience. Learn to believe in yourself and have faith in your abilities. Be unwavering and endeavor to meet your goals. If you fail, you fail. Move on. Understand the obstacles and adjust your behavior to realize your potential. If you quit, you will know what it was like to quit, but you will never know what it is to succeed.

FOCUS

IGNORE THE NOISE.

This challenging world is full of criticism, and some people will look for any chance they get to point out and analyze your flaws. Stay focused and put an end to the negativity. To really get things done, acknowledge the noise around you, but don't let it derail you. As an avid fan of the Pittsburgh Steelers, I have always admired coach Mike Tomlin's ability to focus on the task at hand and not be distracted by the mounting pressures and distractions that are part of coaching in the NFL. His ability to limit the urge to engage in the noise around him has sharpened his focus and boosted his productivity.

How do you stay focused? Eliminate distractions and time wasters. Do you jump into your inbox every time the "new mail" icon appears on your screen? Close your email even if it is just for an hour. The world will not end if you wait an hour or two to respond. More importantly, you will be able to focus on your task at hand. Conversely, real emergencies will come up, and we have to deal with them. However, the majority of situations that come up to distract us are not emergencies and do not require us to respond right away. Many of these will resolve themselves on their own with time. Responding to these requests immediately will only set you up for more replies. By not responding, you're sending a message that you are a focused person who is very busy.

A great example of focus is writing this book. Four practices that I employ when writing are getting a good night's sleep, working offline, designating a perfect writing spot and devoting specific hours to writing. One of the main symptoms of chronic sleep loss is poor concentration. Getting a solid seven to eight hours of sleep ahead of a busy workday could be the difference between being frazzled and being laser-focused.

If you can disconnect from the Internet, there are fewer things to distract you. Experts believe that every time you flip between tasks,

STARVE THE DISTRACTIONS AND FEED YOUR FOCUS.

whether it be responding to a friend on Facebook or checking your inbox, a little bit of your attention remains with whatever you just left. According to a concept called *ego depletion*, we have a limited amount of mental energy, and both decision-making and willpower can drain it. To save that energy for concentration, proponents of the theory suggest getting rid of excess variables that require you to make decisions, like choosing where to work. Try working from the same location whenever you need to focus. That way, when it's time to get the work done, you won't have to waste time deciding where to go. We've all been there. Moreover, give yourself tighter time parameters by maintaining "focus hours."

There are many ways you can cultivate focus in your everyday life that will yield a better, healthier and more peaceful world. I have never paid attention to my critics, but instead forged ahead without the fanatical digital interactions of email, texting and social media. I make significant progress that way. Enter the fear of missing out (FOMO) that pervades young, as well as adult, mindsets. In small doses, FOMO can be a harmless fixation. In excess, it can translate into more dangerous outcomes. FOMO has become widespread in society. Teens and adults continue to text while driving because the possibility of a social connection is more important than their own lives and the lives of others. They interrupt one call to take another, check Facebook and email when on a date because something more interesting or entertaining just might be happening.

The biggest challenge we face related to focus is not distractions, but rather our lack of clarity. Many of us have been told what we should be doing instead of knowing what it is we must do. Focus is deciding what is important and never taking it for granted. It isn't about how well we use our task management systems or apps or how fast we can blaze through a pile of emails. Focus is not about the dignity of meaningful work and starting to define productivity differently. It's about taking time away from all the noise and asking ourselves challenging questions about our roles in life, our values and our dreams. Our life's vision and values are at the very foundation of meaningful productivity. Focusing on who we are and who we want to be in our character, values, vocation and relationships are all paramount to adding value.

FRIENDS

**ONLY THOSE WHO CARE ABOUT YOU
CAN HEAR YOU WHEN YOU'RE QUIET.**

Friends are those who know us better than others do, people we can count on when the need arises. Yet how much time do we invest in those people who matter more to us than all the other people we meet and interact with throughout our lives, sometimes including family? A good friend encourages us, tolerates our shortcomings, accepts us unconditionally and cares for us no matter what. A real friend walks in when everyone else is walking out. A good friend knows you sometimes better than you know yourself and isn't afraid to tell you things you don't want to admit to.

Good friends are important to your mental health and the quality of your life. At the beginning of this book, I mentioned a special group of friends christened the Crazy 8's. While marriages, children, careers, interests and extended family constantly impact the daily structure and flow of our lives, our friendship is an opportunity to love and open up to the full experience of life. Friends take time and attention. You need to call them, text them and make an effort to be with them. We live in a world where technology makes it very easy to communicate. So, be proactive and keep in touch regularly. Whether with a short message or a brief phone call, it's nice to know you are in your friends' thoughts. These little things could really brighten up your day. You have to be willing to let them get to know you, and it has to go deeper than just the superficial stuff. Respect them enough to allow for disagreement in your relationship, and allow your friends the freedom to be different from you without criticism. Friendships can and do change. One minute you're doing things with another couple who are empty nesters like you, the next they are babysitting grandchildren. Be flexible and adapt to different ways of relating to each other.

Another incredible impact of friendship is the meaning your friends give you. I feel honored when the people I'm close to in

SOMETIMES FRIENDS CAN CHANGE OUR OUTLOOK, WHICH INJECTS EVEN MORE MEANING INTO OUR LIVES.

my life need to lean on me, and it's a great, great feeling when I've made a friend's day even slightly better. These friends teach you about yourself without even realizing it; they build your confidence with every moment you spend together. The significance of your friendships is something that really can't ever be explained, especially when it comes to the best of friends. The cliché *they know me better than I know myself* really is the best way to explain the meaning of friendships we hold so close to our hearts. Friends, in general, see us and love us for even our quirkiest of traits. They give you reasons to keep going when everything else seems to be going against you.

We all make mistakes, and true friends do not judge; instead, they try to understand our motivation. Additionally, they do not bear grudges or harbor resentment. Naturally, misunderstandings do arise, and it's important to speak up to clear the air at the earliest opportunity. If tackled properly, such incidences will help you get to know each other better.

Spending time with friends fills up our lives with great conversations, heartfelt caring and support and laugh-out-loud fun. When we fall on hard times, friends are there to put things into perspective. Our friends are down-to-earth, positive people who help push us out of our comfort zones while still providing a safe emotional space for us to totally be ourselves.

Friendships will come and go over the years, which can be healthy. Letting go of long-term friendships that have gone sour can undoubtedly be difficult, but when it comes down to your own well-being, these decisions need to become a priority. So be grateful every day for all those friendships you have built, and don't take them for granted. Always make time to remind the people closest to you how much they mean to you.

The value of friendship is undeniable, and it should never be underestimated.

FUN

**LIFE IS ABOUT USING THE
WHOLE BOX OF CRAYONS.**

The last time I heard someone say, "I don't have time for fun, I have work to do," they were taking down their holiday decorations. I also heard some say, "Why worry about having fun? I have too many other things to worry about." Yikes! I always thought the reason you need to have fun in your life was obvious, but to many, it is not. Fun means letting your hair down and relaxing. It means letting go of your problems and worries for a short time.

Our society rewards busy, and sometimes we prefer to pack our schedules so we don't have time to worry or think about too much. Unfortunately, busy also means no time for fun. Fun is important and offers many benefits. It helps us to connect with each other. My family and friends enjoy telling stories long after a shared meal is finished. It's not uncommon for all of us to be sitting around the table laughing at stories from our youth, swapping most embarrassing moments or revealing silly mistakes we've made over the years. We also play board games that induce transparency, which at times is more compulsory than easily expressed.

Conflict is inevitable in long-term relationships, which is why fun is so valuable. Research by Dr. John Gottman has found that couples are happier in their relationship when the ratio of positive to negative interactions is 5 to 1. For every disagreement, misunderstanding or hurt feeling, couples need five positive affectionate, caring or fun interactions for counterbalance. This may sound obvious, but in real life lots of us are not having fun together. How much fun do you have? Do you make it a priority to be playful and positive? When was your last date night with your partner? When was the last time you went out to a movie, went bowling or rode go-karts? When was the last time you went to an amusement park, fair or carnival and actually rode a ride together?

Let's face it; we're all busy people. With our jobs, housework, school, appointments and other daily commitments, finding time to

ADULTS ARE JUST AS IN NEED OF SOME FUN AS CHILDREN ARE, AND THE WELLNESS GAINS ARE NOT DIFFERENT.

play is often a low priority. We overlook it, viewing it as an unnecessary or guilty pleasure. Playtime is not just for kids! Something to consider is that the opposite of play is not work; it's depression. It is imperative that you find time to play. Many adults struggle with the concept of letting themselves have fun, especially when there are other pressing matters at hand.

Think about fun differently. Allow yourself a little fun every day, even if it is something as small as working on a crossword puzzle or watching a rerun of a favorite old sitcom. Find a friend who has playful tendencies. Do something new that you've always been curious about. Because we found out in the last chapter how much value a friend adds, make sure there is at least one fun friend, someone who is adventurous and willing to explore new activities. You may end up being the voice of reason when they want to try something crazy, but try not to dismiss their suggestions. Be open to all possibilities.

Don't underestimate the value of having fun. Yes, it'll make you feel better, but it's also contagious. Your happiness will radiate and inspire others. I don't know where your fun might take you, but I am reasonably sure when you try something new you will be challenged, maybe even scared a little and stretched beyond your limits. Most importantly, you'll be gratified beyond belief. Having fun will probably make this world a much better place, but we'll never know unless you do make time for it. So open the box and start coloring – and be sure to use every crayon.

GENEROSITY

**GREATNESS IS WHAT YOU GIVE,
NOT WHAT YOU HAVE.**

Generosity comes in all shapes and sizes. It is not just about giving to those who are in need, though. It is just as important to give freely to everyone. Our friends may need a word of encouragement or appreciation. Someone might need the gift of being listened to, or someone might just need to be understood. People who are generous in spirit are willing to appreciate those they may not even agree with on some issues. We can add value by showing generosity in many different ways. Generosity is simple, kind and readily available. It's about giving 100% even when you don't have to. It's about treating people the way you want to be treated. It's about taking care of people without expecting anything in return.

In many ways, we seem to have become a more selfish, self-centered and even unkinder society. Numerous people rarely go out of the way to help one another without wondering, "What will I get out of this?" Companies that we once believed were there to support us have placed more emphasis on the bottom line than serving the greater good. Even many social media interactions have become cold and often threatening. Either we will come together in the spirit of compassion or we will completely disappear into an "everyone for themselves" abyss. Nonetheless, all is not lost. There are also many who have been awakened. Call me the ultimate optimist, but I have witnessed more and more people who want to make a difference in the world. They are asking, "How can I be of service?" As I watch the many retirees who choose to volunteer in ways that impact the world and help those in need, I am encouraged by their generosity.

Being generous will free you a little from the burden of materialism. Have you ever noticed that the more stuff you have, the more it taxes you mentally? When you own more, you have more to take care of, more to clean, more to fix and more to replace. On the other hand, if

GIVING GENEROUSLY OF YOURSELF WILL ALSO HELP YOU GROW AS A PERSON.

you had fewer material goods, you'd have more time for relaxing or productive activities. Materialism will have less of a grip on your life.

When you give to another needy individual, you relieve them of a little of their worries or troubles. Perhaps you give to a volunteer organization that takes care of orphans. Even a meager gift can help out dozens or even hundreds of people who are less fortunate than you.

Another benefit of being generous is that you will be less self-centered. You'll spend more time worrying about those you donate time, money or goodwill to and less time worrying about yourself.

It'll make you feel good, too. You should not, of course, give to satisfy your own ego. Such a motive is selfish. The irony is, those who give receive. In letting go – of money, time or material goods –

we improve our own lives. This is not just philosophical or religious teaching; it's a sociological fact. The generosity paradox can also be stated in the opposite. By hanging onto all we have, we lose out on greater things we might have gained. Opportunity and generosity open the same door. Give!

GRATITUDE

THE SECRET TO HAVING IT ALL IS KNOWING YOU ALREADY DO.

A growing body of research suggests that maintaining an attitude of gratitude can improve psychological, emotional and physical well-being. At Thanksgiving dinner, many families will join hands and take turns saying why they are thankful. In our family, everything from pumpkin pie to iPhones and from family to friends are part of the discussion. Imagine what might come up if we shared our thankfulness at dinner every day and turned a holiday tradition into a way of life. I am continually reminding myself of how fortunate I am for all of my blessings. Being grateful also helps overcome negativity and our tendency to dwell on problems, annoyances and injustices rather than upbeat events. Adopting a more upbeat mindset also helps facilitate gratitude.

Instead of bonding with friends over gripes and annoyances, try sharing why you're grateful. Focusing on blessings can help ward off depression and build resilience in times of stress, grief or disaster. Make thankfulness a daily habit. If you find you take too much for granted, try to imagine what life would be like without a significant blessing, such as a spouse, a child or a job. Gratitude is good for you. Studies show grateful people are happier, healthier and better able to withstand hardship. It is not happy people who are thankful. It is thankful people who are happy.

Being grateful doesn't imply you've got rose-colored glasses on permanently. Likewise, it doesn't mean that everything is necessarily wonderful. It only indicates that you're aware of your blessings, appreciate small things and acknowledge all you do have. A lot of times we take for granted everything that's great in our lives and dwell on what we perceive is wrong. Maintaining an attitude of gratitude takes practice and persistence. When something bad happens, it's easy to revert to internal negative language such as, "Why do things like this always happen to me?" Make a conscious

> # BEING GRATEFUL IS A MATTER OF CHANGING THE LENS FROM WHAT IS MISSING TO WHAT IS PRESENT.

effort to switch from focusing on the obvious negatives to why you are thankful. You find a blessing in a flat tire by appreciating it could have been something more serious. Chances are that when you are faced with a challenging situation, you can find a benefit – or shall we say silver lining?

Years ago, I took a lot of things for granted. I never realized how much value gratitude added until I found myself broke, friendless and hopeless. I learned a lot about the importance of having gratitude during that period in my life. However, it's easy to be ungrateful these days, to want things we don't have. In fact, it is woven into the fabric of our society. Everywhere we turn, we're reminded of what we don't have by someone bragging about what they do have. Social media provides a platform for people to show off where they have been, what they have done and what they have purchased. As I stated in my book *Enjoy The Ride*, people purchase things they don't need with money they don't have to impress people they don't even like. When you work tirelessly to get ahead in life, and even endure some failure or financial struggle, it's easy to be dissatisfied and ungrateful.

We have all been there, done that and have the bumper sticker. Many positive people have overcome adversity by realizing that gratefulness is quite possibly the most direct pathway to success. The problem is that too many people hinge their happiness on the decisive achievement instead of the expedition. When you learn to be grateful along the journey, it adds so much value. It softens trials, changes perspective, elevates attitudes, focuses attention, redirects negativity and empowers us to see more clearly, as well as expands, widens, lifts and deepens our sense of meaning and purpose. Not only do trials teach us new things, but they also add joy and meaning to daily living. So be grateful for all your experiences during your stopover on this great planet called Earth. Drop to your knees and thank God for the opportunities you have been afforded to learn at the feet of life's challenges. Our trials are, after all, among the greatest teachers, mentors and benefactors. Be grateful.

GROWTH

**ONLY THE WALLS YOU BUILD
YOURSELF CONFINE YOU.**

Change is inevitable. Growth is optional. We tend to think of our champions and idols as superheroes born different than we are. It is sometimes uncomfortable to think of them as ordinary people who made themselves extraordinary. At my 40th high school reunion, I was approached by a classmate who, during our high school years, was on the student council, participated in every sport offered and was in the top ten academically. That evening was a reminder of how some people persistently develop, while others struggle to embrace change and move beyond their comfort zone. He said, "Steve, I didn't see you as a person who would end up being an accomplished author and speaker. You just seemed like a regular guy who had a knack for making people laugh. Funny, here you are doing what you do, and I ended up working in the steel mill, living in the same town and never really living up to my title as *Most Likely To Succeed*. Funny how things worked out."

The reality is that we all dream of living a life filled with value and purpose, yet in today's fast-paced society it is incredibly easy to become complacent with what we have and what we know. There are always opportunities and ways of improving yourself. Personal development includes activities that improve your awareness and identity and develop talent and potential. You must continually take an active role in figuring out what needs to change or what needs to be improved in your life. Working in a steel mill and living in the same town is just as terrific as any other situation as long as it fulfills your preferred purpose. That's what matters most.

Everyone is unique, and the pathway toward growth and development is a personal journey. We are all *wired* differently, which explains why "things work out" the way they sometimes do. It is up to the individual to figure out which pathway is theirs and where it leads. Here are several questions to help guide your growth: *What is*

PERSONAL GROWTH IS AN ONGOING PROCESS OF SELF-DISCOVERY AND IS CRUCIAL TO ACHIEVING SUCCESS IN EVERY AREA OF YOUR LIFE.

your current state? What are your strengths, weaknesses and habits, good and bad? Are you happy with where you are and what you are doing?

What is your desired state? Examine what it is you hope to improve about yourself and why it is important for you to develop those characteristics. Determine how *you* want things to work.

What do I need? Determine what knowledge and experiences need to occur for you to get closer to your desired state. Find resources that are useful toward achieving it.

What is a plausible timeline? Growth doesn't have an age limit; however, make a list of activities that need to occur and what your timeline is for achieving them.

When you start looking at yourself honestly, you will discover things you didn't know. You listen to your own thoughts, feelings, beliefs and desires. You become more self-aware and more true to your nature, which improves your focus and effectiveness. You begin to see things you hadn't noticed before: how far you've come, how far you have to go and how much you can help others. You see and appreciate your value and potential. You discard what is not authentically you. Clarity of who you are and what you are passionate about will emerge. Knowing your passion will spark a calling in your heart. This calling will lead you to walk on your path of purpose. Once you get the taste of knowing what you want to achieve, it will no longer be "funny how things work out." It will be intentionally caused by personal growth. Seeing what you can become inspires you, and growth develops self-motivation that creates momentum.

HONESTY

**IF YOU WANT TO BE TRUSTED,
TELL THE TRUTH.**

Integrity is choosing your thoughts and actions based on values rather than personal gain. Honesty is staying true to yourself and your values even when you're faced with serious consequences for the choices you're making, like losing your job or marriage. It is non-negotiable! When we live our lives with integrity, it means we let our actions speak for who we are and what we believe. Honesty is a choice we make, and it's a choice we must keep making over and over again. It's arriving at the crossroads of choosing between toeing the line or stepping over it. It's about weighing the cost because even the smallest action can have an impact on our integrity and, ultimately, our reputation. It seems like a lonely place to be for those who do the right thing without the backlash, yet it sure feels good to live and work with honesty. When we become known for this highly valued trait, our lives and our careers can flourish.

No matter how poorly you think someone will react when you tell them something, rest assured that they will be more upset when they find out that you lied to them. Not only that, but sometimes the lie can cause much more dismay than honesty, like telling your children that their grandmother "went to sleep" instead of letting them know she died. If they're young, they may end up terrified of going to bed for fear that they'll never wake up again, and if they're older, they'll be furious with you for patronizing them. Some couples stay together for years after they no longer have feelings for one another because neither party has the guts to be honest about the situation. They miss out on time being happier either alone or with someone else. One man I know discovered, upon his father's death at age 90, that the poor man had spent his entire life in a loveless marriage because he never had the courage to tell his wife he was gay. Had he been honest to both himself and his wife, she could have been with someone who loved and cared for her, and he could have lived his life in a way that made him happy as well.

THE WORST TRUTH IS BETTER THAN THE BEST LIE.

Honesty is not always an easy thing to share, nor is it an easy thing to hear. We don't have to agree with what the other person is saying, though, just as they don't have to agree with us. However, to be respectful of the other person's feelings, and to honor the relationship enough to be willing to hear the person out, allows for healthy, mature growth. If, after the truth has been heard, no compromise can be found, then it's time to move on. Bless the other person on their journey and turn the page. This will free up space in your life for more like-minded people to now enter. Most of all, you have respected your own heart by being honest.

It takes courage to be honest in any relationship, and sometimes choosing the right timing helps. But what sort of quality is it if one person carries so much power and anger that the other person cannot express themselves? I have found honesty to be one of the most liberating elements in my life. It lets go of unhealthy situations, associations that are no longer healthy for my well-being and allows beautiful, mature relationships to blossom and grow to new levels. As I suggest in my book *Hide Your Goat*, sometimes you have to break up with your "friends." None of us are perfect, and we may not always like what others have said, or even what we have said, but at least we earn or own respect by having the courage to express our feelings.

Honesty and integrity form the foundation of fully functioning people. Without them, every other virtue will topple. The goodness of someone is directly related to the presence of honesty, which earns them respect and trust. Even if being honest may hurt us in the short term, it will always pay huge dividends in the long run. It can potentially solidify a partnership, boost our self-image and reputation, and attract good karma. You'll find that life becomes a whole lot simpler, lighter and enjoyable when you have a clear conscience, free from guilt, fear or worry. We come into this world with a clean slate. We're born uncorrupted and innocent. We can turn back to this purer state of being if we are willing to peel back all the layers and allow honesty to add value to our lives.

HUMILITY

**PRIDE COMES
BEFORE THE FALL.**

Humility doesn't mean thinking less of yourself. It means thinking of yourself less. In an earlier chapter, I discussed personal growth as necessary for becoming a better person. If we can't accept our weaknesses, then it may be difficult to improve. The person who denies weaknesses may not take responsibility for negative behaviors and may not strive for self-improvement. The first step in becoming a better person may involve assessing our weaknesses. The second step may include a plan for self-improvement. A significant sense of humility may be essential to achieve these steps.

One of the most important human characteristics is humility, yet most of us fail to show it. In fact, with the advent of social media, we do the opposite. We brag and boast through posts and photos, sometimes staging what we share to display a false public persona. From the close-up picture of a lavish emblem on the steering wheel of a car we're driving to the image of a new designer handbag, we try to elevate ourselves. Most people see through the façade. I know I've had my fair share of bouts with an utter lack of humility. So why did I do it? Why did I feel the necessity to brag or show off? Why couldn't I show more humility? When I look back on it today, I realize I was self-centered and suffered from low self-esteem. As hard as that is to admit, I could never imagine going back and being that person again.

I made several changes that helped me to become more humble. The biggest thing I did was listening more. I recognized that because I didn't have all the answers I needed to glean more knowledge from my experiences. I also took the time to say "thank you" for little things. It is one thing to be grateful for something; it is another thing to go out of your way to express that gratitude. When you let someone know how much you appreciate a gesture for tending to the little things, it lets them know you don't take anything for granted.

IT'S HARD TO APPRECIATE WHAT YOU HAVE WHEN YOU'RE FIXATED ON WHAT YOU WANT.

While I hope I've always been considered to be thoughtful, I made a concerted effort to put others at the forefront of my thoughts and statements. It is amazing how much value you add to yourself and others when you start sentences with *you* rather than *I*.

Humility adds value when you become more grateful for what you have, rather than merely desiring the things you don't have. Wanting is not bad; it's just a matter of priorities and focus. The problem with many of us is that we want what we don't have. We are products of a society that promotes money and fame above all else. It's okay to have those things and more as long as you approach the world with humility. The humble person who genuinely appreciates what they have and focuses on others is, in fact, far more likely to be content, happy and successful. Success doesn't make you happy. People who are humble, and therefore grateful, approach success happily rather than trying to succeed to be happy. When you are driven for the right reasons, you will find a peace of mind that is only accompanied by humility.

Humble people add value to the world. They look beyond their immediate needs and consider the needs of others. Adding value isn't about donating; it's about giving more to people than they expect in return. People who show humility in the workplace concentrate on adding value to the lives of their customers and coworkers. They make recommendations and try to help in any way they can, something that boastful individuals don't attempt to do.

When all you care about is being recognized, you're not focused on adding value. In fact, you're doing just the opposite. You are looking for what people can give you or what value you can add to any exchange in an effort to keep up appearances and continue your boastful ways. If you want to add value, keep silent and let your success be your voice. Stay humble!

HUMOR

THE MOST WASTED OF ALL DAYS IS ONE WITHOUT LAUGHTER.

Laughter indeed is the best medicine when it comes to keeping us feeling physically, mentally and emotionally young as we age. Current research has indicated that humor, specifically laughter, counteracts the devastations of stress on the body and immune system. So, it's obvious to me that a sense of humor would ease stress. It is also possible to take things too lightly. We all know the frustration of having a problem that a loved one will not take seriously. We also know people who treat life like a joke and never get it together. This kind of humor usually masks a situation or emotion one doesn't want to deal with or is too heavy to handle.

Many of us underestimate the value that humor adds to our lives. Some are born with a humorous demeanor, while others adapt and make their trip through life enjoyable. Regardless of age, background or gender, humor is one thing that can unify us all and generate a positive and happy atmosphere. Then why do we sometimes pout and infect other people with negativity rather than smiling, laughing and increasing positivity? This journey is supposed to be enjoyed in the true spirit of happiness, regardless of the events going on in our lives.

As a speaker, I have always believed that if you are laughing, you're listening, and if you are listening, you're learning. I also believe that humor creates perspective and balance. It relaxes you. Laughter causes you to breathe deeper, feel better, take risks and occasionally consider the outrageous. Making people laugh always makes me feel better, too. Speaking is therapy for me, and I am often energized as much as, or more than, my audiences.

Aside from the health benefits of laughter, which are numerous and significant, having a sense of humor can provide a way to bond with others, alter your perspective and stabilize any unsettling occurrence. It all starts with a smile. If you can put a smile on your

WHEN HUMOR IS A PART OF YOUR LIFE, IT REDUCES ANXIETY AND FEAR.

face, the laughter will come more easily, and the stress will decrease more rapidly. Sometimes you need to take a step back and reassess the situation by looking at it through a new lens. People continually ask me where I get my humorous material for my presentations. Just observe life and find humor in a situation. I have always had the ability to appreciate the absurd, and instead of allowing it to annoy me, manage any situation through the humor it offers. Trust me when I say, after thirty-five plus years of traveling, I have observed just about everything conceivable.

I was taught to surround myself with a character of people I want to resemble. Enter my Crazy 8's friends. Whether it is in the moment or a story communicated later, people who can make you laugh in the midst of frustrations are priceless. Getting your friends on board can help you find humor in life. Additionally, take time to read humorous books or watch sitcoms and funny movies. The best entertainment can take an everyday situation that is universally frustrating and make it funny.

Life has become increasingly complicated and stressful for many of us, which has made laughter infrequent. As you have learned, laughter is a powerful antidote to stress, pain and conflict. Nothing works faster or more dependably to bring your mind and body back into balance than a good laugh. Humor lightens your burdens, inspires hopes, connects you to others and keeps you grounded, focused and alert. It also helps you release anger and be more forgiving. With so much power to heal and renew, the ability to laugh easily and frequently is a tremendous resource for surmounting problems, enhancing your relationships and supporting both physical and emotional health. Best of all, this priceless medicine is fun, free and easy to use.

In a nutshell, attempt to be fun, interesting and humorous when you're interacting with people. Memorable interactions that create emotions create value.

INTUITION

**YOU KNOW THE TRUTH
BY THE WAY IT FEELS.**

The value of insightful people is immeasurable. They have an ability to understand and recognize a situation before it is evident to the rest of us. For some, this sudden understanding is described as an epiphany. For others, it's what happens when intuition tells the intellect where to look next. Apple founder Steve Jobs once said that intuition is more powerful than intellect. As it turns out, Jobs was onto something.

Intuitive people slow down enough to hear their inner voice. Before you can pay attention to your intuition, you first have to be able to hear it over the noise of your busy life. You have to slow down and listen, which often requires seclusion. You have to march in your own parade, follow your inner voice and listen to your gut feeling instead of immediately dismissing or doubting it. I am not suggesting that you abandon your analytical or critical thinking skills; I am only asking you not to reject your hunches so quickly. This will require you to nurture your creativity. The Mona Lisa and the Sistine Chapel were not the result of a paint-by-numbers kit where all you had to do was put the right color in the right space. They were the result of an ingredient called intuition that guided their creativity. When you start getting that sick feeling because your instinct is at odds with your analytical mind, you sometimes have to trust your gut. You don't have a paint-by-numbers kit, but you are equipped with a powerful mind that, when guided by intuition, can help you make better decisions.

Many of us have fallen into the trap of listening to and being guided by our minds (ego) more than our hearts (intuition). When our ego predominantly rules us, we tend to operate from fear, doubt, judgment, anger, jealousy, impatience and anxiety.

On the other hand, when we are spiritually aligned with our authentic selves, operating from our hearts and in tune with our

> # WHEN WE'RE FEELING DISCONNECTED, DISSATISFIED AND ALONE, IT'S USUALLY BECAUSE WE'RE NOT STRIKING A BALANCE BETWEEN OUR MIND AND OUR INTUITIVE VOICE.

higher selves' knowing or intuition, we tend to make better choices. And when we make choices based on love, we incur more positive and less negative karma. Karma is simply the process of cause and effect. If you do A, B will happen. Karma is essentially the same thing as the law of attraction. When we continuously put negative energy out into the universe through our thoughts, feelings, words and actions, we attract more of that negative stuff back. The reverse holds true as well.

While it may sound like something only mystics and fortunetellers have access to, the truth is there's nothing elusive about it. Intuition is the inner knowledge we all possess if we're open to listening to it. But oftentimes we don't because, as mentioned above, our intellect gets in the way. "Intuition is something that provides understanding and judgment without any rational justification," said psychotherapist and life coach Alla Branzburg. "This is why a lot of times we're not listening to our intuition because we're trying to justify it rationally, and you won't find the justification. So we write it off as irrational and illogical, and a lot of times we're missing out on a very important skill we possess." That's not to say that all of the sudden flashes of judgment we experience are actually our intuition at work. In some cases, what we may think is intuition are actually our emotions screaming messages at us.

Intuition is often misunderstood because we are misreading what we are feeling – we don't know if a message is our intuition or if it's our fear or anxiety. Sometimes that's challenging to interpret. If you have anxiety, chances are your intuition is a little bit harder to get to or to listen to. You don't really feel strong emotions with intuition. It's more like a caller that says, "By the way, pay attention to this." There is little sense of anxiety, worry or urgency. It's like an inspiration, the value of which is quite amazing.

KINDNESS

**BE THAT PERSON WHO
MAKES EVERYBODY
FEEL LIKE SOMEBODY.**

The Golden Rule asks that we treat others the way we want to be treated. Although in today's world that may sound somewhat wishful, you would think that it wouldn't be necessary. Wouldn't it be kind (pun intended) for everyone to inherently understand why kindness adds so much value? While it's acceptable to have a bad day now and then, people seem to have become more rude and inconsiderate. Yes, I am guilty of wielding testiness toward a loved one and strangers when I am frustrated. I am constantly trying to bite my tongue and be more conscious of others' feelings. We all have our own issues, but we need to realize that being mean gets us nowhere fast. If anything, it takes us backward and demonstrates weakness.

Just like negativity, kindness is contagious. Ever since I was a child, I have always enjoyed making someone's day. I want to be the reason someone has a smile on his or her face. As an author and speaker, there really is nothing more rewarding. As a son, brother, father, husband and friend, it is my definitive contribution. I always remind myself that, for everyone I meet, I know nothing about a battle they may be fighting. When I pull out of my neighborhood, I see perfectly manicured lawns surrounding beautiful homes with expensive cars in the garage; still, the people inside deal with tests and trials. The outward appearance of something can be misleading. Likewise, the outward appearance of an individual, whether it is their facial expression, the clothing they wear or their weight, usually initiates judgment among viewers. Unfortunately, I believe we are very quick to judge.

Every year, on the 13th of November, World Kindness Day is celebrated. Shouldn't we practice it every day of the week all year round? Let's start practicing by killing ourselves with kindness. That is correct. I didn't say kill *them* with kindness. I said kill *ourselves*

BEING AWARE OF HOW YOU TREAT YOURSELF WILL DETERMINE HOW YOU RELATE TO OTHERS.

with kindness. Notice sometimes how you talk to yourself. Do you berate yourself in ways you would never do to a friend? Are you highly self-critical? There are many acts of kindness you can direct toward yourself, from taking a day off from work to do nothing but pamper yourself to merely taking a walk in the neighborhood and talking to people you encounter. It takes time to change your attitude toward yourself and others, but it begins with becoming aware of your feelings and thoughts. Just notice how you relate to yourself and others throughout the day, then ask yourself, *Is it with kindness or not?*

All too often, we hurry through activities so focused on the outcome (Destination Disease) that the interaction along the way is missed. From your spouse to the barista at Starbucks, we frequently ignore the opportunity to relate to others. How we relate is much more important than the things we do. If we can learn to give our full attention to how we treat others and ourselves, we might find that the results we so clearly pursue are less important than the road we travel along the way. I have lost count of the number of times I have discovered a moment of true happiness in a brief encounter with an Uber driver, a convenience store clerk or some other seemingly inconsequential encounter in life. When you begin to notice these, you understand the probability for kindness in every happenstance and how much value it adds to others and yourself.

The more kindness we show, the more likely we are to continue showing it. The implications for our children are important. If we teach our children to be kind, not only will they be happier, they will be more likely to share happiness. If we focus on teaching kindness, things like bullying, teasing and other hurtful behaviors decline. In reality, children will be unkind sometimes, so we need to help them process their emotions and learn from their mistakes. After all, they learn how to deal with challenging behaviors by watching us.

There's never been a time where the world needs kindness so much. Focus on kindness. It will lead us all to greater places.

LISTENING

ONE OF THE BEST WAYS TO PERSUADE OTHERS IS WITH YOUR EARS.

Adding value comes down to listening. Take the analogy of designing a car. The manufacturer wants to create a new car. It might be that they want to build one just like some others they've built before, or they may want to build something unique that will outperform anything they have. To really add value, the manufacturer must understand what the consumer wants. The average buyer isn't obsessed with the structural engineering of the chassis, the blueprints for the engine (unless you're Chris Porter or Nicky Boninfante) or the details of the wiring harness. They're likely very interested in how it will look, how much it can carry, how fast it will go and how much it will cost.

Just like some people are better writers than others, some people naturally are going to be better listeners than others. To survive in business, you'd better be listening to your customers and employees. Good listeners seek to understand and challenge the assumptions that lie below the surface of every conversation. Listening adds value when you are willing to have a conversation and then challenge long-held and cherished assumptions. Just because something has always been done a certain way doesn't mean there isn't a different or better way to do it. Attempting to fix something that most people don't see as broken isn't popular. Doing something different adds an unknown risk to a venture. However, there is also a risk when you close your mind to new ideas. If you always take the position that you know what's best, you stop listening and miss opportunities to discover something better.

The best listeners recognize that they cannot succeed without seeking out information from those around them. When you show respect for other people's ideas, they're more likely to reciprocate. They are also more likely to continue to share their ideas, which fosters growth and increases the likelihood of success. Listening

THE BIGGEST COMMUNICATION PROBLEM IS WE DO NOT LISTEN TO UNDERSTAND. WE LISTEN TO REPLY.

also involves drawing out relevant information to help uncover fresh ideas and solutions. I have found that when something goes wrong, the more I actively listen and ask respectful questions, the better chance I have of uncovering solutions. It's worth mentioning that asking respectful questions does not mean that the questions can't be tough or pointed. I take pride in being known as a person who is firm but fair. The key is to ask questions in a manner that will promote, as opposed to hinder, the free flow of communication and idea generating.

Want to become a better husband, wife, parent, neighbor and friend? Start acting like a leader; stop talking and start listening. Being a leader should not be viewed as a license to increase the volume of rhetoric. Wise leaders know there is far more to be gained by surrendering the floor than by dominating it. In this age of instant communication, everyone seems to be in such a rush to communicate what's on their mind instead of realizing the value of everything that can be gleaned from the minds of others. Show me a person who doesn't recognize the value of listening to others, and I'll show you a train-wreck in the making.

Listening, real listening, is a skill – and one that can be learned. Being a good listener is more than nodding quietly while someone talks or being supportive. It is *active*. You focus, you pay attention, you clear your mind of your own thoughts. For example, sometimes in conversations, I feel myself formulating a response when someone else is talking. When I do that, I am not really paying attention to what they are saying. I also have a bad habit of getting impatient and interrupting someone before they are finished expressing their thoughts. I am continually trying to respect the person talking and hear what they are saying. Like any other skill, it takes practice and endless self-reminders.

The true listener is more effective, learns more and does more good. So try listening. Listen to your wife, your husband, your father, your mother, your children, your coworkers and your friends. Listening is an opportunity to learn something new, try something old and overcome frustrations. Old angers and resentments can be overcome. All of us want to be listened to, and all of us want to really be heard.

LOVE

FOR IT IS IN GIVING THAT WE RECEIVE.

When you hear the word *love*, most people think about the feelings they have for their family and friends. Maybe you think about your favorite food, sports teams or beverage. Some use the word to describe the feeling and respect they have for their country. In the English language, love can apply to all of these things and many others. So, when *love* is used, even as the title for a book chapter, you have to consider the context to understand how it adds value.

Most people believe that love is a formidable factor in happiness. However, is the determining factor the person receiving or giving? Many psychologists suggest the need to love is a prevailing element of happiness. If so, then how come many of us aren't aware of it? If you were asked what would make you most happy, shouldn't your response be serving others? But, too often the response to that question is money or being loved. In my opinion, the answer has to do with the messaging to which we are routinely exposed by our culture. These messages suggest to us that our happiness lies in being the recipient of another's attention, love and respect rather than being the donors of attention, love and respect. We are shown that happiness lies in achieving self-enhancing goals such as career success, wealth and social status. Conversely, the need to care for others is rarely emphasized, except perhaps in the arts or special events that draw attention to helping others. As a person who attends a lot of charity events, I can attest to the fact that the same people attend the same events annually. For some, the reason for attending is more about the benefit of being seen than the benefit for the cause.

Regardless of your intent or interpretation, this world needs love. Love can bring sources of positive energy to a discouraged soul or broken heart. Love can beat sadness, pain, anger, envy, revenge, challenges and suffering. No one inhabiting this earth can live a

LOVE IS IMPORTANT BECAUSE IT CAN KILL A THOUSAND WORRIES WITH ONE SMILE, WITH ONE HUG.

happy and fulfilled life without love. The problem is that not many people spread love in the right way. The advent of social media allows people to text "I love you" instead of saying it in person. They share loving quotes on the Internet without expressing any real feelings. People need a warm hug instead of an emoji. Children need love to grow, not the latest device. It's time to say I love you instead of typing it.

Love is important because it gives you the strength to fight your weaknesses. It helps you survive bad times with a smile on your face. It enables you to fight every negative emotion that shouldn't exist in your life. Love can fight the entire world. Love is important because it brings people together. It stays on your side forever, even after the person you loved is no more. Love stays with you when you're defeated, only to make you stronger and try again. Love makes you hopeful. It makes you believe in happily ever after. When you're single, you wonder if you're ever going to meet your soul mate. Love makes you know that it is possible, and when it happens, it's really, really amazing. Love makes you fearless. The things you used to fear disappear when you love and are loved. You know you have your own personal cheerleader in your corner to help you with whatever is needed. You almost feel protected because you're in love.

Love is the grease that allows the wheel of life to continue turning. For when we love, we look beyond ourselves, beyond our needs and desires. We sacrifice our time, our energy, our wishes and sometimes even ourselves because of love. It is love that allows law enforcement and emergency services personnel to face danger. It is love that allows soldiers to risk everything. Love makes heroes every day in every corner of the world.

The ultimate definition of love is not about feeling good, but rather about doing good. A perfect example of love in action is Mother Teresa, who worked so long and so hard on behalf of others. It indeed is in the giving that we receive and add value to others and, in turn, to ourselves.

MISTAKES

NEVER BE DEFINED BY YOUR PAST. IT WAS JUST A LESSON, NOT A LIFE SENTENCE.

For many of us, our most significant growth in life has come by making mistakes. You would then think that instead of fearing or hiding from them, we would embrace them. But isn't that what all self-help books and motivational speakers tell you to do – turn your blunders into opportunities? Yes, but unfortunately, the sometimes slanted perception social media projects makes people fall prey to the idea that when we make a mistake, we have a problem instead of an opening. We look for pity, support and a parallel opinion. Instead of a mistake providing a platform for learning and taking more risks, it offers a stage for drama.

I believe mistakes are important, must not be underestimated and are a vital and timely component to our ability to learn. At our company, it might seem counterintuitive, but mistakes are addressed positively, and employees are given the confidence they need when they make mistakes. We try to create conditions for our employees to succeed and recognize that with success, of course, comes trial and error. Knowing that works, it's how we function best. It's not that we encourage mistakes, but rather support them and find value in their misgivings. We believe it encourages us all to try harder the next time with even more resolve and determination. I firmly believe our employees are less inclined to make mistakes because they're not afraid of them. They understand the power of creating a culture that recognizes their importance.

Mistakes can help us change deeply embedded norms and keep us humble. It was discovered in aviation, for example, that accidents sometimes occurred because junior pilots were afraid to correct more senior pilots when they mishandled problems. The same is true in fields such as medicine. By examining why those accidents happened, experts figured out ways to develop more flexible hierarchies, which creates better work environments overall. When we think we're

AN ENCYCLOPEDIA OF MISTAKES MAY BE EVEN MORE HELPFUL THAN A DICTIONARY OF GOOD IDEAS.

above making mistakes – or that others are – we stop questioning and challenging. That can lead to complacency and awful decisions. Bill Gates said, "Success makes a lousy teacher. It seduces smart people into thinking they can't lose." Overconfidence leads us to be blind to the limits of our expertise.

Focusing on mistakes can be difficult, especially when they are your own. After all, most of our mistakes are painful reminders of times when we messed up. Why would I want to look back at a divorce that left me crying and emotionally paralyzed for a year? What good is going to come from that? Examining that divorce would tell me exactly why it all fell apart. In this case, it was because I knew what was important, but took it for granted. Our relationship was never going to work because I was fundamentally flawed and ignored those flaws until it was too late. Unfortunately, I ignored those mistakes, and that proceeded to sabotage my next relationship. When we let our failures and mistakes fade into the atmosphere, we make it harder to succeed. We lose track of the factors that make the difference between succeeding and failing. We start losing critical information, such as *What caused this to fall apart? Why were we defeated?*

One of the greatest lessons you will learn from making mistakes is forgiveness. With every mistake you make, you will learn how important it is to forgive yourself and many of the people around you. You will understand that you are not perfect and that perfection doesn't really exist, only our intentions of doing our best with no regrets.

Speaking of regrets, believe it or not, if you play it safe you will have more and more regrets about the things you did not do rather than the things you did do, and you will regret not making more mistakes. Personally, whenever I hesitate to do something because of the fear of making mistakes, I imagine myself looking back at my life on what I have achieved and realize that if I don't take action, I will have regrets.

You gain confidence, courage and experience every time you make a new mistake. Remember Thomas Edison? He failed more than a thousand times while working on the light bulb, and in the end, his mistakes made the world a brighter (pun intended) place to live.

MOMENTUM

**EVEN IF YOU FALL ON YOUR FACE,
YOU'RE STILL MOVING FORWARD.**

Momentum has an integral part in the field of physics; however, many people do not see the importance of momentum in everyday life or even recognize it. From driving a car to hitting a baseball, momentum is crucial. When we keep moving forward, we thrive. When we stop, we stagnate. When something is moving, it can be a lot harder to stop it. Equally, when something is not moving, it can be a lot harder to get it going. If a four-wheeler with no one driving is rolling down a hill, stopping it would be problematic. If a four-wheeler with no one on it was not moving at the bottom of the hill, to get it rolling up the hill would also be problematic. Ill-advisedly, I have been there, done that! However, it serves as a great example of how momentum adds value, and the more we have it in our lives, the easier our lives will be.

There's a positive reaction when you keep taking action. As soon as we give up, regrettably, we tend to focus on the last result we got, which was negative – unless we keep adapting, keep adjusting, keep learning and keep trying. With each incremental step, we gain more confidence for the next attempt. We'll know more, know what not to do and have a greater chance of achieving our goal. As in the previous chapter, it supports why mistakes add so much value. We are momentum-based beings; therefore, we have to focus on getting started, even if it is a small action (reread the Action chapter). Movement is the key. Without it, we have to build everything up gradually, which takes more effort than it would otherwise. When attempting to get motivated, half of the battle is won by just getting started. A big part of the other half is won by keeping on keeping on.

Once you have momentum, you will get into a rhythm with the task you are doing, and it will become easier to perform. As many a sports broadcaster has said, when you have "the big Mo" on your side, it is important to maintain it. The wonderful thing about momentum

IF YOU HAVE DONE SOMETHING FOR A WHILE, THE LAST ACTION YOU TOOK WILL PROPEL YOU ONTO THE NEXT ONE.

is that there may be times when you fail to get what you are aiming for, yet you still wind up unexpectedly getting something else that was just as good. I believe these unforeseen events occur as a result of positive momentum that is previously set in motion. Bearing down, doing the work and establishing momentum creates opportunities. Once you experience the benefits of momentum, motivation is no longer a problem. You begin to see the positive results that come from it. When you step on the scale and see you have lost two pounds, positive reinforcement will give you the confidence and the motivation to keep dieting.

Persistence, in turn, gives you endurance. If you continue to exercise, you will eventually lose weight and inches. To gain momentum, get started, stay consistent and surround yourself with people and influences that can keep you on track during those times when it is hard to keep going.

A real-life example is writing this book. Each day, I gain a certain type of momentum. Every day, including today, there is something that says, "Writing time!" However, then something unexpected happens, like a phone call that focuses my attention on something that needs to be repaired or otherwise tended to. I can assure you it will be harder to write tomorrow, but the more experienced I have become, the more I realize I don't like losing momentum. Hence, I am sitting here in a hotel writing so I can keep "the big Mo"! I can attest to momentum's true power, and it's wonderful.

So, figure out what you love and desire, set some goals and start gaining momentum.

OPTIMISM

WHEN IT RAINS, LOOK FOR RAINBOWS. WHEN IT'S DARK, LOOK FOR STARS.

W here do I start, and where do I end? As I began this undertaking, I listed over 100 things I believe add value to people, products and services. With the help of a focus group, we narrowed the list to 52. Optimism was a strength that was at the top of many lists. From developing fewer physical illnesses to overcoming setbacks, the presence of optimism lets us build ambitious goals and dreams that keep us motivated and focused on their achievement.

Optimism comes from the Latin word *optimus*, meaning "best," which describes how an optimistic person is always looking for the best in any situation and expecting good things to happen. Optimism is the tendency to believe, expect or hope that things will turn out well. Even if something bad happens, like the loss of a job, an optimist sees the silver lining.

In life, we are often presented with situations that are less than ideal. Whether those are challenging times, people or circumstances, most of us can relate to coming up against roadblocks that feel hard, unfair or even devastating. We can help transform our challenges into opportunities by viewing them through a new lens and assigning the right value to them. The lens we view our world through is as individual as we are. We don't see the world as it is; we see it as we are. Limited vision and a perceptual bias create a constrained reality. When we practice looking at life from different viewpoints, it becomes more natural to feel compassion for others and ourselves. Perspective allows us to realize that the glass is half empty or half full depending on whether we're pouring or drinking. With perspective, we can come closer to finding the silver lining in just about any situation.

Joel Osteen said, "Nothing happens to you; it happens for you. See the positive in negative events." It's natural to feel helpless and mistreated. However, if you look at things as happening for you,

WHAT WE SEE AND BELIEVE TO BE TRUE IS NOT "THE" TRUTH, BUT "OUR" TRUTH.

then you take some of your power back. It is vital for us to judge the importance of something correctly. We have to assign the right value to the situation. Doing so gives us inner strength that makes moving through challenges more fluid. Assigning the right value means that if we don't like something, we change it; if we can't change it, change the way we think about it. Manure is just manure by itself, but when used constructively, it is beneficial to life.

Fortunately, you can change your thinking patterns over time, and if you change the way you think, your life will change forever. Even a pessimist can become an optimist with enough practice. All you need to do is reframe how you define events. Instead of dwelling on the bad experience, analyze it to figure out what good can come of it. If a project at work is deemed a failure, think about what you learned during the process. What strengths did you discover within yourself, and when can you use those talents again? Instead of blaming yourself for the failure, think about the outside influences that may have affected your project. It isn't about looking for excuses; it's about turning the situation into a learning experience to increase your potential for success in the future.

Optimism is a skill of emotional intelligence, which translates to a better career and greater success. Life is too short to be made miserable, so start changing the way you think. Many of us are under the impression that opposites attract. Although this may be true for magnets and couples in bad romances, when it comes to spirit, the opposite is true. Like attracts like. In its simplest form, this means that if you learn to harness the power of positive thoughts, you will attract more positive circumstances. What I have learned is that if you are looking for something good or beneficial in a person or situation, you will always find it. While you are searching, you will become a more positive and cheerful person.

Resolve today to learn how to develop positive thinking and a positive attitude toward yourself, the people around you and your life. Optimism can advance your prospects for work, relationships and other life experiences.

ORGANIZATION

**FOR EVERY MINUTE
SPENT ORGANIZING,
AN HOUR IS EARNED.**

Everyone has a bit of chaos in their lives. Schedules, deadlines, traffic, children and numerous other responsibilities all seem to demand attention at the same time. Being organized can be a valuable resource that helps us navigate our way through it. Above anything else, organization will reduce your stress level. I am married to a woman who, like me, believes in keeping closets, attics and all of our belongings organized. I'm willing to guess that, generally, most people are not very well-organized. The good news is that organized people are made, not born. Organization is a skill that anyone, in any profession, can learn and use to increase productivity and efficiency. For many, becoming organized is related to getting rid of paper and clutter, improving their filing system or finding more time each day to get things done. However, there is another facet that really is the basis for solving all of these problems: being in control. That means you are in control of how you handle paper, email, social media, your phone and all of the responsibilities and distractions that make up your day.

Getting organized is more difficult than it initially sounds. You seemingly have more questions than answers. How organized must you be? When do you know you're organized enough? Do your clothes need to be hung according to color? (If you're me, yes! ☺) What are the most important areas of your life to organize? Where do you start? I believe the two most critical areas are your house and your time. A cluttered home can subtly drain you of energy and cost you money. You don't need to alphabetize your books and line up your shoes by color, but it is essential to have a place that makes sense for everything. Wouldn't it be nice to finally park your car in the garage? If you find yourself continually rushing and have trouble shutting off your mind from everything you have to accomplish, chances are you are stressed out. Getting organized can make a significant impact on your life. When you're not worrying about what you forgot to do,

ORGANIZATION ISN'T ABOUT PERFECTION; IT'S ABOUT EFFICIENCY, REDUCING STRESS AND CLUTTER, SAVING TIME AND MONEY AND IMPROVING YOUR OVERALL QUALITY OF LIFE.

and clutter isn't occupying your thoughts, you will be more aware of what you need to get done – and magically do it.

I would not be where I am today if it were not for my organizational skills. As I climbed the corporate ladder, I rapidly learned how to prioritize and delegate to people and other departments. I had to become organized in how I did my job, or I would have sunk. When

I was ascending in leadership, Bill Gates and Steve Jobs hadn't yet delivered Microsoft or any smartphone technology. It was called a typewriter, pen and paper. My former secretary, Margaret, always said, "There is today, tomorrow and next week. File, focus and finish them accordingly." If only she had lived long enough to exploit these folders on a desktop in Outlook. I would have also appreciated her opinion on how to unbury myself from my inbox. One thing is for certain: she would have emphasized to look at what needs to be accomplished today, set deadlines for the rest and set aside necessary time for unanticipated crisis management. She also cautioned me not to try to get everything done in a day. "It will be there tomorrow," she would tell me. She was right! Put those items in your tomorrow folder and make them a priority tomorrow. She always underlined the importance of keeping yourself organized, up to date and, more notably, sane and reasonably stress-free.

So why does organization add so much value to your life? You have less stress, more time to relax and, most importantly, more time to spend with your family. I once saw a bumper sticker that read, "Organized people are just too lazy to search for stuff." While it is a cute saying, I am okay with being the "lazy" one mentioned as the punch line. Less time looking means more time to spend with my wife, children and grandchildren. My Saturdays are not spent stressing out over what needs to be cleaned out, but rather enjoying our four-wheelers in the woods or our bicycles in the park. There is something to be said for drinking a cold beer sitting in an Adirondack chair by your fire pit without that overwhelming feeling of guilt that stands between you and "done."

When you know where things are, what your goals are and take care of things as they come, you will have significantly more time and energy for what matters most.

PARTICIPATION

RAISE YOUR HAND WHEN NO ONE ELSE DOES.

It is easy to blame low levels of participation on apathy and lack of motivation, especially if you're getting frustrated in your efforts to encourage others to join in. As the president of my homeowners association, I used to get discouraged and thought that some residents didn't care about our neighborhood, or that some had paid their dues and felt it was someone else's turn to step up to the plate. However, I knew the importance of participation and was determined to find out why some of my neighbors did not get involved. The principal reasons were the presumptions and attitudes within our organization, starting with my own. I had to overcome my supposition that it would be hard to get people involved because they were always too busy. I recognized that if no one saw me excited and optimistic about their involvement, then they probably wouldn't invest very much of themselves. It is remarkable what happens when you give people the benefit of the doubt and expect the best.

Other reasons we don't participate is because we are unaware of opportunities to become involved or have been ignored when we tried to participate in the past. All too often, leaders of organizations have their own agenda and do not include others in the planning, organizing and decision-making process. If we expect to be ignored, we'll be less likely to offer our services. Some of us may not see the value of participation or don't believe we can make a difference. Also, unfamiliar situations, such as the annual HOA meeting, may cause anxiety. To increase participation, be very clear about what others can expect to happen at the meeting, what they can expect their role to be in the organization and what will be expected of them if they get involved. However, according to a Gallup Poll, the main reason we don't get involved is that nobody asked us. From my experience, when you approach people individually, you let them know they aren't a faceless number in a mass appeal. When we interact on a

WITHOUT PARTICIPATING, YOU CAN'T SUCCEED. WITH PARTICIPATION, YOU CAN'T FAIL.

personal level, especially between friends or neighbors, involvement is less intimidating and distant.

An enormous benefit of participation is perspective. As a business owner, I want to hear your ideas and feedback. Effective engagement is about recognizing that involving people in targeted objectives is no longer about disseminating information and telling others what needs to be done. It's a two-way street of shared ideas. Participation isn't about qualifications; it's about outlook, opinions, thoughts, beliefs and priorities. Hidden agendas and my-way-or-the-highway attitudes have no place. Without perspective, decision-makers might not make the best choices for the whole simply because the loudest voices of the few win out. You know, the squeaky wheel gets the grease. Additional perspectives expand options and enhance the value of the ultimate decision.

Participation also promotes ownership. When you are directly involved, you take more ownership, which is key to a successful outcome, even if not all individuals necessarily agree with that outcome. When you talk to players from successful teams, a common thread is that they play for coaches who listen to what they have to say. They also agree that when the game is over, and you have won or lost, it feels good knowing you were involved in the process.

Participation is a powerful way to maximize your potential and transform a condition. People want to participate, but sometimes are afraid. Remember back to when a teacher asked a question, and you wanted to raise your hand and answer. Your fear of being wrong outweighed the reward of being right. Yet, even a wrong answer would lead to identifying a weakness and improvement. Great leaders invite participation, especially in meetings. Being heard makes employees feel valued. This feedback goes both ways, too. You stand to learn as much from your employees as they do from you.

Participation has no substitute. Keep involving, learning and growing.

PASSION

ANYTHING THAT GETS YOUR BLOOD RACING IS PROBABLY WORTH DOING.

You really didn't think I would write about what adds value and not include the topic of passion, did you? As a professional speaker, one of the questions I am regularly asked is, "How do I find my passion?" My answer often surprises a few people. While I consider it essential to find what ignites you, I also believe it's just as important to cultivate a simple lighthearted attitude of play, wonder and adventure. When you deliberately open yourself to noticing things you might enjoy doing, don't be afraid of getting it wrong. Life is an adventure that allows you to learn and grow as you go. Happiness research shows that trying new things contributes to sustained levels of contentment. In essence, observe what you love, and when you long to have more time for it, chances are, you'll discover something you are passionate about.

Ever wish you could paint? There are painting studios that now offer painting sessions for "fun art," not fine art. You can go with friends, sip your favorite beverage and enjoy step-by-step instruction with an experienced local. Not only can you leave your cares behind and go home with a one-of-a-kind painting that you created, but you leave knowing you tried something new. Just like the "Hey Mikey!" Life cereal commercial campaign that ran from 1972 to 1986, you may be surprised what you end up liking. People are passionate about different things. Some people are passionate about social media, while others are passionate about watching baseball and playing tennis. I'm passionate about passion. It's the energy that keeps us going, that keeps us filled with meaning, excitement and anticipation. Passion is a powerful force in accomplishing anything you set your mind to, and in experiencing work and life to the fullest extent possible. Passion is the driving force that allows us all to live better lives.

We are all unique and special in one way or another. You have notable talents that others do not. Find out what they are and exploit

CHASE YOUR PASSION, AND THE MONEY WILL COME. CHASE MONEY, AND YOU WILL NEVER FIND YOUR PASSION.

them. Uncover your passion, and happiness will follow. Many of us spend our entire lives not exercising the gifts we were given, working in careers we don't like and spending time with people with whom we have nothing in common. We accept jobs for the money, friends for the status and circumstances because it's easier. Doing something we love compared to something we dislike relieves stress and allows us to be more optimistic. When we do something with our heart and soul, it will feel awesome, even if it isn't what everyone else expects us to be doing.

When we're passionate, we innovate, create and continue with our dreams. Every successful person in life begins by pursuing a passion, usually against all odds and the self-serving advice of others. If I had listened to other people, I would still be in corporate America and not writing this book. When I contemplated a new career, instead of encouragement, I received every conceivable scenario of why I would fail. However, the beauty of entrepreneurship is that you have only a passion, a good idea and a dream. Though my path to becoming a professional speaker and bestselling author went a few different directions, my passion never faltered. Ideas and dreams may come and go, but good things will come your way if you have sustained passion. When you display passion about your work, whether building a house as the owner of a construction company or selling the home as a real estate agent, others will see it and be drawn to it.

Life is too short to waste time doing something you're not passionate about. Make sure you are clear about your direction and what your end goal is so you can align your decisions along the way.

Not everyone knows their passion immediately. As I suggested at the beginning of this chapter, try new things and focus on what you enjoy. Find out what ignites that fire in your belly and what skills you possess. The key is to discover what makes you happy and apply it to your personal and professional endeavors. Passion does not necessarily come overnight, but the value it adds will allow you to consciously take charge of your life.

PATIENCE

**WHAT'S MEANT TO BE WILL
ALWAYS FIND ITS WAY.**

Patience is essential to daily life and is one of the keys to happiness. Having patience means being able to wait calmly in the face of frustration. Opportunities to practice it occur every day: at home with our family, at work with our colleagues and everywhere in public that people can find a reason to be impatient and annoyed. Patience, like faith, requires work. As Benjamin Franklin said, "Genius is nothing but a greater aptitude for patience." Isaac Newton wrote, "If I have ever made any valuable discoveries, it has been owing more to patient attention than to any other talent." There are many reasons why patience can have a positive influence in your life and help you to achieve any form of success, from owning your own business to attaining your annual goals. The skill can be hard to master, but the results are worth it.

There is a long list of reasons to be impatient. Telemarketers, long traffic lights, people not taking their turn at a stop sign, long checkout lines at the grocery store, rejection, disappointment – and the list goes on. How do you deal with it all? A new adage needs to be *Frustration Happens!* You have a choice that includes driving yourself silly, behaving irritably, playing the victim or trying to force an outcome. The problem is that these reactions are all self-defeating, alienating and bring out the worst in others.

So, do good things really come to those who wait? In 1968, a Stanford University researcher presented each member of a group of preschool children with a single marshmallow. He wanted to see which of them could resist eating it long enough to earn a second treat. Follow-up studies found the children who'd demonstrated sufficient patience to win a prize experienced greater success later in life. They were more likely than the impatient children to earn good salaries and less likely to suffer from addictions of all kinds. The researchers concluded that those blessed with an ability to defer

FORTUNATELY, EVEN IF WE AREN'T BORN WITH A GREAT DEAL OF PATIENCE, IT'S A VIRTUE THAT EVEN THE MOST AGITATED AMONG US CAN DEVELOP.

gratification enjoy greater life chances as the result. For the majority of us, patience doesn't come easily. When it does, it is often fleeting. We rush, interrupt, squeeze in front of the line, curse slow drivers in the passing lane and charge things now rather than paying cash.

Here are three tactics I employ to build up my patience. First and foremost, I try to reconsider situations and not have an automatic emotional response. For example, when the airline delays my flight, instead of fussing and fuming, I use the extra time to read and write. I see it as an opportunity to accomplish something rather than a waste of my time. Consciously regulating our emotions can help us train our self-control. Traveling as much as I do can test my patience; however, if I am in a rental car, I always – and I mean always – pay the extra $7.99 for SiriusXM satellite radio. When you have to deal with other drivers and the annoyance of traffic jams, it's natural to become anxious. The car I drive to and from the airport has satellite radio. The NFL Network or one of the comedy channels gives me something else to think about, and the distraction recharges me. Finally, I practice being grateful. I have found that if I am thankful for what I have today, I am not desperate for more stuff or better circumstances.

We can try to shelter ourselves from frustration and adversity, but they come with the territory of being human. Practicing patience in everyday situations, like a delayed flight, will not only make life more pleasant in the present, but might also pave the way for a more satisfying and successful future.

A simple and practical way to nurture a stronger sense of patience is to realize that ordinary moments that cause us difficulty, inconvenience, anger, disappointment and so on function as real-life opportunities to practice. And, what we realize through these experiences is that most of our impatience is rooted in a lack of perspective on the events or people that are causing our feelings of angst. If you can't find a close parking space at the mall, focus on the fact you will get the exercise you need. Enjoy the fresh air and put a positive spin on every situation. You will not only reduce tension, you'll become a much happier person.

PERSPECTIVE

ANYTHING AND EVERYTHING IN LIFE IS UP TO INTERPRETATION.

There are over 7.5 billion people in the world; hence, there are a lot of interpreters and lots to interpret. The good news is that some people have similar viewpoints, which unites different people for the same reason. However, the basis for uniting may be for an array of reasons that are not similar. The bottom line is that we need to appreciate the differences in perspective and, therefore, others. By embracing these differences, we can better understand ourselves in ways we can't imagine on our own. The way we see the world is our reality, and it's unique to us and us alone. However, our reality is not the only one that exists. Every person has their own realities based on their view of reality. We can argue and criticize their viewpoint; nonetheless, the truth is that their reality is their perception. The primary reason why perspective adds so much value is that it allows you to look at things objectively rather than picking a side. It's having an open mind and a willingness to learn what someone is going through.

We frequently have tunnel vision and get stuck in our own patterns. When we have a broad mind and attempt to understand both sides of the coin, we grow. There will always be more than two sides to every story. Whereas, knowledge can be obtained by seeing one side, wisdom knows all sides. Right now, someone is questioning how there can be more than two sides. Well, there is your side, my side and the way it really is. I don't read, watch or listen to the news, and feel I am better for it. Besides adding confusion, when you start your day reading and hearing about murders, criminals, disasters and warped people, what kind of a day are you going to have? But Steve, isn't that a somewhat far-reaching view? Is it? Have you ever felt like the car you were in was rolling backward, only to realize that your car was actually still, but the car next to you was moving forward? You inadvertently judged your movement based *not* on what was truly happening, but on what your mind thought was happening.

> # IF THE PATH BEFORE YOU IS CLEAR, YOU'RE PROBABLY ON SOMEONE ELSE'S.

Sometimes what we see and hear are not entirely valid or accurate. Like an optical illusion where what the eye sees isn't accurate, it can be difficult to gain a correct perspective at times.

Many factors can distort reality. When people are under emotional stress, intoxicated, depressed, anxious or lacking sleep, things can seem more significant or out of proportion than they really are. Ever wonder why someone is temperamental or explosive about something you felt was inconsequential? If they are not well-rested or are stressed out, chances are their reaction to a situation is based on imbalanced emotions. This is why texting after you've been drinking is never a good thing to do. Step back from the situation without reacting, and you may find that your perspective has changed drastically. You no longer want to quit your job or post embarrassing pictures or ugly comments on Facebook.

As a business owner, husband, father and friend, I regularly seek the perspective of people I trust. I want to hear their perspective on things that will improve my understanding. More times than not, other people who are not as close to the situation as you have a more accurate assessment. Gaining perspective is something that grows with experience. Having friends and mentors who can share their experience with you is a helpful thing. This is one reason why support groups are so vital for people with addictions, medical issues and grieving. Learning from people who have traveled a similar path can make your journey much easier.

It is extremely important to understand the importance of perspective in our lives, because if we don't, we are severely at risk for misinterpreting much of what is going on around us. As I revealed, I am not a person who reads the newspaper. Nevertheless, I remember asking a gentleman beside me on a flight why he was reading three of them. It seemed like a waste of time and money. His response delivered a perspective I had never thought about. He said, "The three newspapers cover most of the same news, but different journalists convey different things. One focuses on what happened, one on why it happened and another on when it happened. I basically enjoy getting different perspectives of the same issues." Essentially, he was saying the "how" can be as important as the what, when and why. Thus, a great example of why people only understand from their level of observation.

If someone gives you ten dollars, and someone else gives you twenty, before you judge one as more generous, you may want to know that the person who gave you twenty had two hundred, and all the other person had was that ten. When you change the way you look at things, the things you look at change.

PREPARATION

**PREPARE HARD.
FINISH EASY.**

Abraham Lincoln said it best. "Give me six hours to chop down a tree, and I will spend the first four sharpening the ax." Mistakes can often be avoided if you double-check your perceptions. Builders have learned to avoid making foolish mistakes by measuring twice and cutting once. It is a constant reminder that they have one shot to get it right or it will cost them time, money and even reputation. Measuring twice is a good metaphor for decision-making. You need to make sure you think of all the things that could go wrong before acting or making a decision. Many mistakes are due to a failure to clarify expectations about outcomes and processes. Not asking the right questions, not following the process or failing to communicate clearly are a few of the leading causes that precede bad decisions. In other words, as Benjamin Franklin so famously said, "If you fail to plan, you are planning to fail."

As an author and speaker, I am often asked during a media interview to share my secrets to success. My understanding of this question is that typically the interviewer is endeavoring to give their audience a shortcut or foolproof path. There are no shortcuts! Success requires heavy lifting and more lifting to maintain it. Retired four-star general Colin Powell says, "There are no secrets to success. It is the result of preparation, hard work and learning from failure." It never ceases to amaze me when people use the phrase *it must be nice.* What they fail to realize is that notable achievement is always preceded by significant preparation. When singer, songwriter, actress, record producer and dancer Beyoncé was asked how she can sing live and at the same time dance as vigorously as she does, she revealed that she practices her dance routines in heels for eight hours a day. So how committed are you to your craft? I have said to many aspiring speakers, who have sought my advice, that anyone can give a speech; it's the preparation that separates and stops most speakers from going all the way.

TO BE A SUCCESSFUL ENTREPRENEUR, YOU ONLY HAVE TO WORK HALF-DAYS, AND IT DOESN'T MATTER WHICH 12 HOURS YOU PICK.

So what preparations are you making for your success? Are you staying away from dream killers and those who attempt to keep you down in the same pit of non-achievement in which they dwell? Are you ready to wake up early, stay up late and turn down social events just to focus on the preparation required for the success you envision for yourself? Preparation doesn't generally include pleasant diversions such as lunch with a friend, long weekends, boating, golf, social media, texting and talking on the phone – unless, of course, that's how you define your own brand of success.

Unfortunately, many people are simply unprepared and offer up many excuses for why. Most unprepared people say they didn't have time to prepare. Sorry, but if it really mattered, you would make the time to prepare despite everything else happening.

Life is all about preparation. Preparation is all about hard work, sacrifice, discipline, organization, consistency, practicing the right concepts and more. "The will to win is not nearly as important as the will to prepare to win," as the saying goes. Remember Beyoncé? Remember *it must be nice*? Many people want what's nice, but aren't willing to put in the hard work and time required to become great at something. What makes this even more challenging is that preparation is not a one-time event. You can't prepare to win once and then expect success to just maintain its course. Great performers possess the will to prepare to win over and over again. Adequate preparation may not be fun and can often appear to be boring and uninteresting, especially to those of us who love the buzz of the game more than practice.

The good news is that preparation is a skill that can be learned and, with discipline and experience, improved over time. For some, planning and preparation may come naturally. Others meet and deal with challenges as they occur. The difference between being reactive and proactive is preparation. The advantage is that you can manage problems more quickly and efficiently because you will already have the solutions at hand ready to be implemented.

Preparation enhances self-discipline, improves strategic thinking, increases flexibility and develops our resilience. Take a moment to consider how you go about your daily life. Are you missing out on some wonderful opportunities because you are not preparing yourself sufficiently? Do you always repeat the same mistakes because you resist preparation? Add value to your life by preparing for tomorrow by working hard today. Prepare hard. Finish easy.

PRIORITIES

**IT'S NOT ABOUT HAVING TIME;
IT'S ABOUT MAKING TIME.**

We live in an age where time runs so fast that we often deviate from the important tasks to complete less significant ones. There is a direct correlation between your priorities and achievement. A person who does not set priorities is often left tired and confused, chasing any number of things and feeling unsatisfied in the end. That bewilderment makes it hard to be fruitful in any part of life. While setting priorities, try not to give in to the temptation to start at the bottom of your list and work up to the important tasks at the top. Don't major in minors. It's human nature to follow the path of least resistance. We tend to start on small tasks, thinking that as soon as we get warmed up, we will launch into our big tasks and increase productivity. Not so.

Some of us go in a hundred directions at once. While doctors may diagnose this as Attention-Deficit/Hyperactivity Disorder (ADHD), I am inclined to think it is sometimes IDD (Interest Diversity Disorder). My stepson Alex is a great example of a person who is always in pursuit of many interests. He is a jack-of-all-trades and has accumulated knowledge and information about many things. What he has found is that his time and resources are limited, and no activity will impact the direction and progress in his life more than that of setting priorities. We can have all the determination, discipline, motivation and inspiration we want, but if our efforts are scattered or misdirected, they will have little impact. If you wholeheartedly work toward a goal now, then enthusiastically work toward a different goal a few weeks from now, you are not likely to achieve either one.

More often than not, if we are stressed out and fail to accomplish what is important, it's because we have made something else a priority. For some, it can be a job, social media and something as simple as a television series. We have to examine our priorities and decide what's important consciously. If your family is more important than

SETTING PRIORITIES ALWAYS INVOLVES SACRIFICE.

your career, then choose to put more efforts into your family life and understand that your career may not be as successful. At least you are living by your priorities. Your time is limited. Things usually take longer than we think they will. So, to get where you really want to go, choose which roads you are not going to travel down. Decide where you want to end up, set your priorities and determine the sacrifices you are willing to make to get there.

Many of us are guilty prioritizing more than we should at any given time. That creates preventable stress. Priorities can obviously shift, and they *should* shift over time. I've learned that, to make progress and not get burned out, it's important to stick with a small number of priorities at one time. Otherwise, they're not really priorities, are they? It's easy to fall into the trap of being too busy herding the cattle to build a fence. The scenarios we most want to avoid are fixing the same problems over and over again. To stop chasing cows, we need to consider empowering other people, developing processes and even eliminating particular tasks. Look at your to-do list and, before you make an investment of time, decide how you can save time.

To begin adding tremendous value to your life, come to the end of your day and feel like you have met your most pressing needs and accomplished what is primarily important. If you're struggling with prioritizing the important over the urgent, don't be too hard on yourself. It's natural to want to get easier trivial tasks off your list; however, inconsequential tasks have a nasty tendency of taking up more time than they should.

Making quicker decisions can add a lot of value. When you've got a pressing decision to make, don't over analyze the situation. Make a choice, clear out the mental space and move on!

PURPOSE

FIND YOUR WHY.

Some of us live our entire lives trying to figure out the purpose of our existence. When we know our purpose, we tend to live more meaningfully. We live each day to the fullest because we know who we are, where we're coming from and where we're heading. Purpose is knowing why we live. Economics, science, medicine, arts, literature, religion, philosophy and other disciplines at our disposal help us to discover and fulfill our purpose. For some, purpose is about studying, working and raising a family. For others, it may be going on vacations and enjoying many other meaningful activities. While there is no one method for finding your life's purpose, there are many ways you can gain deeper insight into yourself and a broader perspective on what it is you have to offer the world. As I mentioned in the chapter on passion, you have to find out what gets your blood racing. It's what makes you come alive and desire to be something more significant than the current you. It's about connecting the passion with the purpose and focusing all of your efforts on what puts that fire in your belly. This isn't about a declaration that you are going to invent the next big thing in technology. Purpose is connecting to a cause consistent with who you are and why you care. When we launched the Gilliland Foundation, we determined that our purpose was to provide funding that creates lasting solutions for causes that we are passionate about.

When you find your why and follow your passion, the money will find and follow you. Sometimes you only need to look as far as what you are good at. Great products market their brilliance. Purpose-driven people discover their natural talents and come alive when they use them. Knowing your greatest strengths and where you can add the most value can help you focus on the opportunities, roles and career paths where you are most likely to succeed – and therefore find the greatest sense of accomplishment and contribution. You'll tend to

WHEN PEOPLE ARE IN THEIR ELEMENT, THEY ARE NOT ONLY MORE PRODUCTIVE, THEY ADD VALUE AND ENJOY MORE PERSONAL AND PROFESSIONAL FULFILLMENT.

be more successful at focusing on your natural resources and things you're inherently good at than trying to eliminate your weaknesses.

While it is by chance that the chapter on *purpose* follows the chapter on *priorities*, it isn't accidental that living with purpose means focusing on things that matter most. What matter most are rarely "things." Too many of us define ourselves by what we do for a living rather than accepting what we do for a living as just a part of an overall purpose that guides our lives. Once you understand your why, you'll be able to clearly express what fulfills you and better understand what drives your behavior when you're at your best. When you can do that, you'll have a point of reference for everything you do going forward. You'll be able to make more intentional choices for your personal and professional growth. Robert Bryne said, "The purpose of life is a life of purpose." A life without purpose is like going on a vacation without a destination.

People who are purpose-driven have decided to act in the direction of their dreams. A strong sense of purpose fuels their motivation. They have a definite sense of direction and a clear understanding of what success means to them. Everything they do is consistent with their goals. They continually look forward with their sights set on where they want to end up. Their day-to-day activities help propel them closer to their visions. Once you find your why, you will be more careful and selective about your daily actions.

Knowing your purpose may require you to take on challenges that will stretch you as much as they inspire you. When a clear purpose powers you, you increase your chances of succeeding.

RELATIONSHIPS

**ONE OF THE HARDEST DECISIONS
IN LIFE IS CHOOSING WHETHER
TO WALK AWAY OR TRY HARDER.**

How much value do you bring to the table? Do you contribute to other people's lives in a meaningful way? Do you give more than you take? Relationships need to add value to your life beyond someone saying "I love you." After all, how many people do you know who profess their love, but whose actions don't match their words? Do your friends contribute to your life and your goals? Obviously, I am assuming that you want someone to add value to your life. When you genuinely love someone, you value them and see them as equal. In the best relationships, this reciprocal valuation lasts and lasts, but in less than ideal relationships, each person's value in the other's eyes fades, and not necessarily at the same rate.

When you meet new people, you look for common interests. You want to relate and figure out if you'd enjoy spending time together. You also consider whether these people would be a good fit for your other friends. There is a reason why they are called "inner circles." People have to mesh well with different personalities and bring something positive to the table. What do you add to the experience of others? Some add value by being a good listener, empathizing and offering constructive feedback. Friendships can add value by relating and teaching things that someone might not have known. When I look back at our friends (Crazy 8's), it is remarkable how much they added value by getting to know one another.

Relationships add value in numerous ways. Do enough good for people, and they will want to return the favor. This mindset works in social, romantic and professional settings. Adding value to other people's lives without considering how much they add to yours is a one-way ticket to being a doormat. Examine all of your relationships and consider their value.

So, how do we determine what our relationships are worth? What brings the value of a win-win relationship into focus is when you strip

MAKE ENOUGH GENUINE DEPOSITS IN A PERSON'S LIFE, AND YOUR RELATIONSHIPS WILL PROSPER.

everything else away and ask yourself what's important. It becomes readily evident that good relationships are invaluable. When you are building relationships, don't settle for someone or something that doesn't align with your core values, goals and attitude. Over time, my wife and I realized we had relationships that barely added value and consumed too much time from our lives and careers. Meanwhile, other relationships of value to us received less attention than they deserved. We now crave connections that prove to be meaningful on emotional and professional levels and more.

Contributing to other people (adding value to their lives) is the only way to gain another person's buy-in, and it's one of the few ways to get others to believe in you. So again, I ask the question: How much value do you bring to the table? When is the last time you gave a helping hand, were a shoulder to cry on, showed someone a better way, listened more and provided your full attention? No matter how we contribute, always be authentic and never enter a relationship with an ulterior motive. More times than I like to admit, people became my friends for concealed motivations.

In a relationship, adding value or going the extra mile is doing something nice for someone solely because we know it will make him or her happy. When you care about someone, show it. Adding value doesn't have to be high maintenance or expensive. Something as effortless as running bathwater or bringing a cup of coffee scores big points in a relationship. Adding value is listening more than you talk and caring about others. Love yourself, love other people and build relationships that positively impact your world.

RESPECT

RESPECT IS HOW TO TREAT EVERYONE, NOT JUST THOSE YOU WANT TO IMPRESS.

Respect can mean different things to different individuals and cultures. Though the definition may vary, it usually centers on character, experience and ethics. Learning respect often starts at an early age and continues to develop over time. Growing up, we are taught to respect our parents, teachers, elders, school rules, traffic laws, family and cultural traditions, other people's feelings, opinions and rights, our country's flag and leaders and the truth. We come to value respect for such things when we're older. We develop great respect for people we consider exemplary and lose it for those we discover to be dishonest, which may lead us to respect only those we feel are genuinely worthy. We may also come to believe that, at some level, all people are worthy.

What exactly is respect? It's not something you get just because you are put into a certain position. After all, any system is prone to manipulation, from gaining an undeserved position of authority in a company to finding yourself in charge just because there wasn't anyone else around. True respect, according to dictionary.com, is "a feeling of deep admiration for someone or something elicited by their abilities, qualities or achievements." So, you could respect someone just because they are the boss or have amazing abilities, either natural or earned by years of practice. Furthermore, you could respect someone because they can do things you could not dream of doing. Wouldn't it be better, though, if you earned respect because you chose to do the right thing, honor others, walk your talk and stay above the fray.

To be respected, I feel you have to match your actions to your beliefs. Just because you say you are a person of integrity or that you care about people does not make it true. Talk all you want, but talk is cheap. Actions matter. People are watching. Your children are watching. Coworkers watch. Friends watch. If you make bad choices

IF YOU WANT TO BE RESPECTED, ACT RESPECTFULLY.

and never acknowledge your missteps, you will dig a hole trying to earn respect. To earn respect, be polite to everyone – from your spouse and children to your coworkers and to the checkout person at the grocery store. I know, this is easier said than done, especially when you're having a bad day. Just remember: everyone else wants to be respected just like you do. So, open the door for the person behind you, or let the person with one item go ahead of you in the grocery store. Smile and say please and thank you whenever possible.

Eliminate disrespectful behaviors such as rolling your eyes, concentrating more on your devices than on others or talking over someone. Not only are these actions rude to the person you're interacting with, they create a wedge that can become permanent. Instead, foster an environment of respectful listening. Everyone deserves to be heard, even if you don't agree with their ideas or opinions. Consider how you'd like to be treated if you had something to say about a particular issue. To gain respect, be worthy of it. Be a good person – someone who looks for the best in others and follows through on promises. Tell the truth, be transparent and genuinely care about others. Show your gratitude early and often. Respect the people you work with, and they will respect you in return.

It's never too late to start earning respect and adding value. Start by taking an honest look at yourself and how you treat those around you. If people respect you, respect them back. If they disrespect you, still respect them back. Give it to get it.

RESPONSIBILITY

MORE PEOPLE WOULD LEARN FROM THEIR MISTAKES IF THEY WEREN'T SO BUSY DENYING THEM.

A responsible person can be trusted to act in accordance with agreed-upon terms because they are accountable for their own behavior. In other words, when you say you are going to be home for dinner at 6:00pm, you don't make an excuse for arriving at 6:30pm. As a parent, I have always tried to teach four boys to behave responsibly. Responsible behavior has five important components, which are honesty, respect, fairness, accountability and courage. Being fair means balancing your personal needs with the needs of others. It means if your parents are divorced you make sure one doesn't always win over the other. It means not always seeking your own way at the expense of others.

We should learn to acknowledge and accept whatever happens as a result of *our* decisions, actions and mistakes. Blaming others for things we do wrong is both dishonest and unkind. Making excuses doesn't improve the situation. The more excuses we make for bad behavior, the less likely people are to trust what we say in the future. Do what you say, and say what you did. The more you stick to what you know is right, the easier it gets. You'll find it easier to trust yourself to make the right decisions. If you need someone to pick something up on the way home, who are you going to ask?

It is a good feeling when people trust you because they believe you are capable of accomplishing things without any supervision. This boosts your self-esteem and self-worth. As an employee, you soon recognize that you're given tasks and assignments of higher importance. However, as you confront difficult assignments, don't blame others for setbacks or problems. Take responsibility for success and failure. This is where the popular saying *there's no reward in life without risk* comes into play. Responsibility isn't about entitlement; it's about stepping up to the plate acting responsibly. Show me a person who is dismissive with a duty they perceive to be tedious,

PEOPLE WHO TRUST THEMSELVES CAN BE TRUSTED BY OTHERS TO MAKE THE RIGHT CALL.

and I will show you someone irresponsible. Irresponsible people do not follow the rules. Instead, they rationalize their actions and try to convince you why their way of thinking is correct.

When you finally embrace that life is full of choices, and what you make of them determines your outcome, you will recognize that your life is a product of your decisions, which is what accepting personal responsibility is all about. Sometimes you have to swim against the current, and other times you need to go with the flow. Just like we need perplexing situations to teach us patience, we need difficult circumstances to teach us responsibility. Calm waters don't make a skillful sailor. Occasionally, the hardest part is taking responsibility when something goes wrong, Even then, people respect someone who owns up to making a mistake and works to fix it.

Responsibility adds a lot of value. As a responsible person, you show you can be trusted. This benefits you and the people counting on you. You also earn positive self-esteem and usually go further in life because you are outstanding at working independently. Those who can excel without supervision get promoted and are given more responsibility. If you are leaving for vacation, which child are you leaving the house key with?

The most important aspect of taking responsibility is to acknowledge that your life is your responsibility. No one can live for you. You are in charge. No matter how hard you try to blame others for events of your life, each is the result of choices you made. Every choice and action matter.

Making excuses instead of taking full responsibility for actions, thoughts and goals is the hallmark of people who fail in their professional and personal lives. Think and act responsibly to add value to your life.

RISK

GREAT THINGS NEVER CAME FROM COMFORT ZONES.

I am far from being a marriage counselor, and I am not a behavioral psychologist, but I am observant. One thing I have noticed is that people who are remarried tend to be more comfortable with getting outside of their comfort zones. Because risk is usually an expression of your ideas, it can teach you a lot about yourself. When you get married young, I believe you are not as comfortable exploring new abilities within yourself. However, the older you get, when circumstances change, you become more aware of what truly lies inside you. The more success you experience within those areas, the more confident you become. Are there downsides to risk? Absolutely! That's why it's called *risk*. You could put yourself out there in a big way and fall flat on your face. Failure can be a great teacher, however. Evaluate where you are and think about where you want to be, then take the risks necessary to get there.

For me, taking risks and business growth go hand in hand. As an entrepreneur, I take risks, large and small, on a regular basis – not for the fun of it, of course, because that would be irresponsible. The risks I take are calculated and based on an underlying motivator. Generally speaking, I work to differentiate myself from other authors and speakers. With the age of blogging, self-publishing and SEO (Search Engine Optimization), you can go unnoticed if you are not prepared to take some risks. Think of someone you consider to be successful. Chances are, they've put themselves on the line at least once to get where they are.

Taking risks teaches lessons that you can't learn elsewhere. Remember, not every chance you take is going to have a positive outcome, and that is perfectly fine. When you fail, it's lesson learned, wisdom earned. Move on. If you dream big, chances are you will fail more than once. Risk-takers want to achieve more after their actions bear fruit. After writing *Enjoy The Ride,* for example, I was eager to

> # RISK-TAKERS DREAM BIG, AND THAT USUALLY STARTS FROM A PARTICULAR REWARD ATTAINED FROM A PARTICULAR ENDEAVOR.

write something different and travel into new, undefined territories as an author and speaker. Because of the learning and knowledge I acquired through many processes, I was better able to understand what I could and couldn't do. I didn't plunge into writing a new book; I dipped my toes in the water while pursuing the dimensions of the subject matter I was about to explore. After my feet were wet, I went for it.

There is nothing static with risk. Risk-takers acquire more freedom and flexibility. A huge value add of risk is that it helps you define a change or adapt to change. Risk-takers don't get stuck in the ride, but rather move with it and set the tone. Don't get me wrong – doing something different could lead to discomfort and a whole new direction you never anticipated, yet getting out of your comfort zone can bring you to the life you want. As I stated in the last chapter, *there's no reward in life without risk*. Think about it. Try naming one historical figure that made a difference by playing it safe and being average. The vast majority of people who have accomplished significance took risks to make a difference.

Risk-takers are a different breed. Trust me, I know! They are not afraid to live beyond the boundaries, or, as my colleague Jeff Tobe would say, "color outside the lines." There is no such thing as failure, only experiments that didn't work. Risk-takers are marked by a sense of adventure and passion. We are focused on squeezing everything we can out of every moment. As *Star Trek* taught us, risk-takers "boldly go where no one has gone before."

If I only was allowed to give you one piece of advice, it would be to take more chances. Head down the road less traveled – better yet, the road never traveled before. You may get lost and find nothing, or you might discover something extraordinary. Put yourself on the line. Try something new, break the rules and live life on the edge. Not only will you feel much more satisfied, but you'll have some pretty amazing stories to tell. More importantly, you will never have to say "what if?"

VISION

**DON'T LIMIT YOUR CHOICES
TO WHAT SEEMS POSSIBLE OR
REASONABLE. DISCONNECT FROM
DOING WHAT EVERYONE ELSE DOES.**

From the very beginning, Southwest Airlines has been a maverick in the airline industry and customer service area. They set themselves apart every single day through delivering remarkable service by going above and beyond how their competition does it. Their vision and purpose are to connect people to what's important in their lives through friendly, reliable and low-cost air travel. This vision unifies and guides them, and is the reason for their existence and motivation. Southwest's vision sets the course for their success, and knowing how they operate, it should continue leading them down the path to the milestones that lie ahead. They have never taken the approach that they need to do what everyone else does, nor have they ever been afraid to try something new. When you follow the crowd, you will not surpass them. When your vision is to walk alone, you are likely to find yourself in places no one has ever been before.

Quality, cleanliness and service are the core values on which Harry and Esther Snyder built In-N-Out Burger, the regional fast-food chain that counts celebrity chefs Gordon Ramsey and Thomas Keller among its rabid fans. With a per-store average of over $2 million, In-N-Out's revenue figures beat those of the high-profile national chains. Their vision in 1948 was never to be the biggest, only the best. They now have well over 300 locations in six states, and, despite pleas from Wall Street, In-N-Out has resisted IPO and franchising, preferring a steady expansion that lets it maintain a close watch on each store's products and execution.

Harry Snyder's vision not only added value to his brand, but he revolutionized the fast-food approach. Adding spark to his concept, he developed a two-way radio ordering system that let customers get a quick meal without leaving their cars. More than high tech, the high quality of the burgers and fries kept customers coming back.

IF YOU CREATE A VISION FOR YOUR LIFE, DOORS WILL OPEN.

Harry inspected each produce shipment and made sure the lettuce was hand-leafed, with tomatoes and onions up to par, while never serving the end of an onion or tomato on a customer's hamburger. His vision was to pay associates above minimum wage and always pay vendors on time. If a vendor was ever caught sneaking subpar product into a shipment, Harry ended their relationship on the spot. He was fair, but firm. He had the ability to see what was invisible to others. You might even say he was the Howard Schultz (former Starbucks Chairman and CEO) of his time because he wasn't afraid to risk more than others thought was safe or dream more than others thought was practical. To this day, their menu has never changed and consists only of hamburgers, French fries and drinks. Practical?

Harry and Esther Snyder used their vision in two different ways, inspiration and prediction. They first used it to inspire themselves. They also used it to predict changes in the future regarding their interests. A vision might be the most powerful way to keep focused on what you want in life while keeping motivated to achieve it. A vision will open up your mind to many possibilities and a brighter and bigger future. When you can envision a future that is better, happier and more productive, you are more likely to make the changes necessary for you to reach that lifestyle. As is the case with In-N-Out Burger, when a vision is spread through a company, it pushes both the leaders and employees toward the same goals. Vision can successfully turn a corporate hierarchy into a harmonious and well-organized group.

Finding and realizing your purpose is not easy. Everyone telling us what we're good at, how we should live our lives and what careers we should explore can be very confusing. Society has made us believe that the busier we are, the more successful and important we are, which most times is far from the truth. Once you realize your purpose and write down your vision, life becomes less complex. Passion fuels you. Over time, you will begin to see more parts of your vision coming true – until one day when you realize that celebrities are eating your burgers after an evening at the Oscars. Create the life you can't wait to wake up to!

WISDOM

**FOLLOW YOUR HEART, BUT
TAKE YOUR BRAIN WITH YOU.**

If you ask my family and friends to tell you something they have heard me say on many occasions, chances are someone would say, "Lessons learned, wisdom earned." Somebody else may tell you that I have always believed that knowledge is power. Stop the presses! There was a time when knowledge was power because it wasn't as readily accessible as it is today. The Internet has made it abundant. Facts and information are easy to find. Knowledge, therefore, doesn't seem to be worth as much as it once was, especially because it's often difficult to distinguish fact from opinion without doing a lot more research. You'd better have a healthy dose of wisdom handy.

One of the leading causes of a lack of wisdom is not understanding how to apply information we gather to our own situations, circumstances and relationships. Victory still evades many. An abundance of books is available on success and how it is attained. Nevertheless, so many of us are living in frustration, depression and mediocrity. While knowledge and education have their place, wisdom allows us to be triumphant and successful. Knowledge permits us to accumulate and interpret information, but wisdom is the appropriate consumption and application of that information.

Children are frequently "educated" in wisdom by cartoons, movies, television shows, social media, performers, athletes, websites, talk shows and pop culture icons instead of by their parents or the wisdom of the ages. It isn't ultimately the responsibility of schools, but of parents and family groups as well as cultural and faith communities to teach wisdom. We are teaching the most important things to our children. We believe that science, technology, engineering and mathematics will lead to stable careers and a ticket to the good life. Languages are helpful, and you can't go wrong with basic computer programming skills, right? What if we at least expose our children to the wisdom that teaches good judgment and strong

IN A WORLD WHERE PEOPLE SEEM INCREASINGLY UNKIND, DISHONEST AND GREEDY, WE MIGHT WANT TO RECONSIDER AN EMPHASIS ON THAT OLD STANDARD CALLED WISDOM.

character and hope it takes root? Teaching children about humility, love, courage, sacrifice and kindness will help them to grow, prosper and find contentment.

People who have wisdom can handle daily challenges better than most. Wisdom comes by learning and growing from experience. When you have good judgment, you will always be solving problems, seeing better results and moving forward. Great judgment leads to strong character and gives you the ability to impact others positively. When you survive a trying experience and maintain your integrity through it, the wisdom you gain makes you unstoppable and increases your ability to influence others. Lessons learned, wisdom earned. Show me a person with wisdom, and I will show you a person who brings honor to his or her personal and professional life. Rev. Billy Graham comes to mind. Yes, we need mathematics, engineering, technology and all the tools of rational science at our disposal to tackle the issues of climate change, national security, mental health and other important matters that face us. We need more than knowledge to confront the problems that loom and threaten our being. As a society, we need to restore wisdom to a place of honor. Information is not knowledge, and knowledge is not wisdom.

Live an enriched life. Live a protected life. Live an honorable life. Live a beautiful life. Live a life filled with wisdom.

THE VALUE
OF A PENNY

The latest data indicates that picking up small coin denominations is a thing of the past. While seven in ten of adults over 55 admit they would stop for a penny, just 37% of young millennials (ages 18-24) say the same. These same millennials, along with their slightly older cohorts, are more likely than any other age bracket to say they would stop for a quarter, but not anything smaller than that. If a cashier fumbles your change and a few pennies drop to the floor, people often don't take time to stoop down and pick them up.

So what is the value of a penny to me? As I aged, I occasionally questioned my faith to the point of not believing what I said I believed. When my father passed away in 2005, I struggled. Not long after, I was asked to speak for a 200-employee, faith-based company. The affluent business owner who hired me asked my office if I could join him and his wife for dinner the night before the event. When the evening arrived, the couple picked me up at my hotel, and we proceeded to a casual restaurant in the area. As we progressed to the front door of the bistro, the couple stopped short, and I witnessed the man bend over and pick up a penny on the sidewalk. I couldn't help but think of how wealthy the man was, and yet he picked up a dirty old penny from a grimy sidewalk. "I noticed you didn't walk by the penny on the ground outside," I said. "Is this how you have become so wealthy?"

He reached into his pocket and, while laying it on the table, said, "Read what it says." I leaned forward and saw the words, "In God We Trust." He then explained that he didn't become wealthy by picking up pennies, but rather by reminding himself of the words. He said, "I believe that God drops a message to me at times He wants to remind me to keep my trust in Him."

As the late Paul Harvey would say, "The rest of the story." Prior to my mother-in-law Rita Rohde's death, she struggled with her health. As her passing was imminent, my thinking began to relapse as it had twelve years earlier when my father died. However, this time it was worse. After all, in 2005, I was 46 years old, and now I was one year shy of celebrating my 60th birthday – just twenty years younger than my mother-in-law.

I was in Houston, Texas when I received the call that she had passed away. I was overcome with a sadness I had never experienced. That evening, I ventured out of my hotel room to eat dinner at a Cheesecake Factory restaurant. While waiting to be served, I began to cry uncontrollably. It was then I shut my eyes and asked God to reassure me that I would see Rita again. After eating a couple of bites, I paid my bill and continued back to the hotel. Before entering the front door of the Marriott, I looked down and saw a scruffy penny face up. It read, "In God We Trust." Within a few days, my wife and two stepsons made our way to Fond du Lac, Wisconsin for a memorial service at the local cemetery. I would be lying if I said that I wasn't still troubled about my belief in seeing Rita again in the afterlife. The night before the service honoring Rita, we went out to dinner as a family and were joined by three other relatives. At that dinner, I leaned over and let my wife know that I was going to find an ATM so I could pay cash for the seven of us who were dining. An employee informed me that the machine was located by the restrooms. As I slashed my way through the crowded bar area and finally found the ATM, I walked over. On the floor, precisely positioned in the front center of the machine, was a penny face up.

When I now find a penny, I pick it up and remind myself of how much value Rita added to her friends, neighbors, family and circumstances. Some people have suggested that pennies are from heaven and are tossed to you by angels. Whatever your belief, or skepticism, the truth is that Rita Mae Rohde added value to my life while living and strengthened my faith through dying.

The next time you see a penny, remind yourself of the message and ask yourself, *When is the last time I added value to someone or something?* I challenge you to become aware of the things that add value and begin to develop an outlook to enhance yourself and everyone you encounter.

Rita Mae Rohde, thank you for adding value to so many people, and for all the pennies you continue asking God to send my way.